ESCAPE
TO
IKARIA

D1634732

About the Author

Nick Perry spent his childhood in rural Dorset. He was educated at Parkstone Sea Training School and left at fifteen for a job at ATV Television in London. He then travelled around Europe for a while and moved from job to job back in London until he came into a small inheritance. On impulse, he and his brother bought a hill farm in North Wales, which is where *Peaks and Troughs* takes place. After seven years living on the breadline, he took his family on a new adventure and 'escaped to Ikaria'. He now lives with his wife in Wiltshire.

ESCAPE TO IKARIA

All at Sea in the Aegean

NICK PERRY

First published in Great Britain in 2017 by Polygon, an imprint of Birlinn Ltd.

West Newington House
10 Newington Road
Edinburgh
EH9 1QS

www.polygonbooks.co.uk

A CIP catalogue reference for this book is available from the British Library.

ISBN 978 1 84697 376 5
eBook ISBN 978 0 85790 940 4

Typesetting by Studio Monachino

Printed and bound by Clays Ltd, St Ives plc

To Arabella

The events in this book happened forty years ago.
The truth is as accurate as my memory will allow.
The names of several characters have been changed.

Prologue

In 1969, my brother Jack and I inherited a small amount of money and bought Dyffryn, a hill farm in North Wales. It was one of those life-changing moments when a decision is taken and wild youth doesn't give a second thought to what lies on the road ahead. We were in our early twenties. I was married to Ros and we had baby twins, Sam and Lysta. We were blissfully unaware that the theory of farming was quite different from the practice. But we did eventually manage to achieve a life of self-sufficiency, living off the land.

The constant struggle to keep ourselves financially afloat soon had us going to the bank to borrow money. We knew nothing about livestock but bought some sheep anyway, and Jack became a shepherd, helped by his beloved Meg, a border collie. We raised pigs and sold them to the abattoir as porkers, before realising we would be better off selling our meat door to door. So every Friday I drove a Morris van around the villages and managed to start making a living. We found out about farming the hard way, struggling bruised and battered through a comedy of self-inflicted errors.

Then Chicago Vomiting and Wasting Disease decimated the pig herd, the only case of its kind in North Wales. After surviving for seven years, we saw it as a sign to move on. The cycle of our farming days had come to an end. But what to do next presented itself in the most unexpected circumstances when I had to have a tooth filled.

Sitting in the dentist's waiting room, I pulled a magazine from the pile, flicked through the pages and came upon an article called 'Hidden Greece'. The few photographs showed a way of life that I could hardly believe was still being lived. Panniers of grapes carried on the backs of donkeys, past whitewashed houses in a landscape of cypress trees under a bright blue, cloudless sky. It was probably the endless drizzle of a winter's day in Caernarfon and the ending of a stage in our lives that made those images so appealing. It was such a random happening – the magazine was over two years old – yet it would set us on a very different course.

We needed a new beginning, and the possibility of living on a Greek island seemed real. We sold the farm, paid off our debts and made our plans, which included organising the children's education with their primary school and being given the curriculum and books they would need for the year ahead.

And so Ros and I, with Sam and Lysta and our youngest son Seth, just two years old, set off to Athens on the 'Magic Bus' from Victoria coach station. The tickets were twenty-five pounds each and the journey took three days and two nights, all of which we spent sitting in hard, upright seats. Where we would end up living, and for how long, we hadn't a clue.

1
End of a Journey

If there's such a thing as 'coach lag' then I had it, leaning slightly to the right, having resisted the tight turns of the bus for two thousand miles. I was revved up and exhausted, a part of me still on the journey. I kept seeing sheep blocking roads, shepherd boys walking behind, waving sticks. Not on the Welsh roads where our journey began, but through Yugoslavia and into Greece. We wouldn't try that back home, moving sheep without a dog. The boys just stood and stared, watching us inch our way through the flock, the driver continuously sounding his horn.

And now here I was, wide awake, walking along the quayside of Piraeus harbour, trying to decipher the Greek alphabet. One letter resembled a cactus plant, another a half-eaten sandwich; my favourite was similar to a hump-backed bridge. It was impossible to even guess the names of these boats, but some stood out in English, *Sea Spray*, *Moon Rising*, *Helen of Troy*, poetically named expensive yachts, all swaying gently in the swell.

The seagulls were wide awake too, or perhaps they just couldn't sleep because of the street lamps throwing a fluorescent light over the harbour. The smell here was very different from the mountains of North Wales: a mix of bilge water, diesel and fresh sea air.

I didn't know what I was looking for, maybe a sign to show me the direction we should be taking. It was nearly midnight in February and I'd left Ros and the children sleeping in a room we'd rented above a café, weary from three days of travelling. Ros and I had managed to walk the children up the stairs and watched them collapse on to the unmade bed, already half asleep, food barely touched. We removed their shoes and threw an eiderdown over them. Ros too was soon fast asleep, still wearing her head scarf.

And here I was, twenty-nine years old with calloused hands, staring at life while it stared back at me. That's how it felt out here in a displaced night, searching for a new adventure. It seemed the only changes I was capable of were dramatic ones.

There was no one about; stars quivering, water lapping, ropes slackening, restless seagulls hopping from boat to boat. But I was not alone. Suddenly someone shone a torch straight at me, the light strong enough to make me put both hands over my face.

'*Poios eisai* . . . *ti kanis?*' someone shouted.

Whatever he was saying, I replied, 'I'm English. I'm looking for a ferry, the next boat going to one of the islands.'

'*Ochi tora.*' Not now.

'When?'

'*Avrio*, tomorrow morning at nine o'clock.'

'Going where?'

'Ikaria.'

'*Efkharisto*,' I said, thank you, one of the few words I knew.

I'd never heard of Ikaria. Maybe it was just a small island, with only a few people living on it. That would suit us, rather than somewhere overrun with tourists in the summer.

It was too late to try to get any sleep, I'd be the worse for it, so I found an empty bench and dozed, clouds smudging out the white lozenge of a faint moon. My hands were stuffed in the pockets of a woollen overcoat, the same coat I'd worn walking the hills looking for stray sheep. I closed my eyes and shut out the remains of the night, smelling the harbour, listening to the gentle slosh of the water.

Some time after dawn I woke Ros and the children from a deep sleep, all of them huddled together in a single bed.

'There's a boat leaving at nine,' I told them as I opened the curtains to a blurred sun rising in a watery sky. In the window opposite, a man in a vest was shaving, two pigeons on the roof above him fighting over a scrap of bread. Nearly every TV aerial had a resident seagull scanning the waterfront.

We walked to the harbour, all of us, apart from Seth, with rucksacks on our backs, me carrying two suitcases. We sat in a café perfectly positioned to see the closed ticket office with the Greek flag fluttering on its roof.

None of us had managed a good night's sleep, but the emaciated cats under our table looking for food distracted the children from their tiredness. Already dock workers were unloading boats, boxes of fish piled high on their trolleys.

Ros and I tried to wake up on cups of Greek coffee, those small ones with an inch of sediment in the bottom. A couple of sips and you'd finished it. Bleary eyed, we watched the port of Piraeus coming to life. Despite a breakfast of yoghurt and honey, Sam and Lysta, our seven-year-old twins, made it perfectly clear they would rather be back in Wales. Already, whilst on the bus, Lysta had written a letter to her best friend Eleri telling her how unhappy she was. Seth, meanwhile at the ripe old age of two, was happy to be on his mother's lap chewing a piece of rock-hard dry toast, something I later learnt was called *paximathi*.

As we sat there, fishermen and porters smiled at us warmly. They seemed bemused to find a foreign family huddled together in the early morning having breakfast in a workers' café. Some came out of their way to ruffle the children's hair, accompanied by a strong smell of the sea . . . or was it the scent of the morning's catch that wafted over us? I wasn't sure whether it was curiosity or a genuine sympathy they felt; we were plainly out of place on a dockside in the middle of February, looking like refugees in transit.

I had a thousand drachma in cash and five hundred pounds in travellers' cheques stuffed into the money belt round my waist. I preferred not to plan ahead, but wanted to be prepared for the unexpected and hoped it was enough to keep us going for a while, until I found some work and we could make a life for ourselves.

As I paid the bill, I asked the café owner if he could tell us anything about Ikaria. He seemed astonished and, in what little English he could muster, said, 'You go to Ikaria? You no go there. Nothing in Ikaria,' shaking his head in disbelief.

'Dad,' said Lysta, and I could tell straight away that one of her acute observations was coming. 'What haven't you noticed yet, but when you do will make you cross?'

'I've no idea.'

'Look at the suitcase and rucksacks.'

'Oh, bollocks!' They were covered in seagull droppings.

'Dad, you promised you wouldn't swear in Greece.'

'Sorry.'

'We don't have to take the first boat that's leaving,' said Ros, fearing we were going to end up on a deserted island with no electricity or running water.

'I've got a good feeling about the place,' I said, although I hadn't. I just wanted to get the journey behind us. 'Besides, we can't walk around Piraeus harbour all day avoiding seagulls and trying to keep the children occupied.' I could imagine nothing but frayed tempers.

So I went to the booking office, which had just opened, and bought the tickets for Ikaria. It wasn't until I had handed over the money that the heavily mascaraed woman with bright red lipstick and neatly tied neck scarf told me the journey was going to take eight hours. She reminded me of a glamorous nineteen-fifties air stewardess, like those on the old travel posters. When I told Ros we'd be on board until five in the afternoon it didn't go down too well.

'What's the weather forecast?'

'Force eight gale.' I shouldn't have said that. It wasn't funny.

The children had never been on a boat before. 'You know they'll get seasick.'

They didn't, not for the first six hours. We had the whole upper deck to ourselves, apart from a couple of priests whose grey beards swung in the breeze. Unfortunately, every time Sam and Lysta ran past they offered them sweets from a paper bag. At this time of year, the ferries carried mostly cargo, all the necessities the islands had to import from the mainland. There were more crew than passengers, and they broke the monotonous journey by constantly fussing over us and taking turns to practise their language skills. A lot of them had relatives scattered around the world, especially in America and Australia.

It was the petty officer who painted a picture of Ikaria for me in perfect English, describing it as a remote, out-of-the-way place, not on the tourist route, close to the much larger island of Samos near the Turkish mainland. He told us that during the civil war the government had exiled thousands of communists to Ikaria and many still lived there. Apparently, a lot of Ikarians flourished well into their nineties. He wasn't sure why; perhaps it was the fish diet, or the islanders' custom of lining their stomachs each morning with an egg-cup of olive oil.

The crew, when they weren't hovering around us, seemed to spend most of their time smoking and leaning over the side flicking their cigarette butts into the sea, so the children were a welcome distraction. They took photographs of each other holding them, and gave Sam and Lysta a tour of the whole boat.

'Your children are blond like the original Greeks.'

I said to Ros, 'I hope it's not always going to be like this, everyone treating our offspring as if they were young gods.'

The captain, too, must have been at a loose end and invited us onto the bridge. 'British built,' he said, fondly patting the dashboard in front of him. 'Solid and secure.' Then he proudly announced, 'I left my wife for this ship. I fell in love with the engineering.' He was another one who couldn't understand why we were going to Ikaria.

'What will you do there? It is cold in the wintertime. No people, no fun. Yes, come in the summer, lovely beaches, but now no, it is madness.'

I didn't have an answer to that. Instead I asked him if I could steer the boat for a while.

'It's a ship, not a boat.'

But he let me take the wheel, and in the calm waters of the Aegean Sea I took control of the ferry.

I sang 'A Life on the Ocean Wave', but he didn't seem to appreciate it.

Suddenly I found myself alone on the bridge. For whatever reason, everybody had wandered off. Beneath me were thousands of tons of steel; I was overcome with the feeling that I was Jack Hawkins in *The Cruel Sea*. But it didn't last for long, as the captain reappeared, offering me a *souvlaki*.

I was surprised when Ros said we had been at sea for over six hours. Until then the weather had been fine, blue skies, gentle breezes, seagulls following us. And then Petty Officer Ianis, who I was now on first names with, announced there was a storm brewing. Sure enough, clouds started to gather, the wind strengthened, and coffee cups slid across tables as the ferry began to roll from side to side. They told us to go below where the ship's movement would not be so severe.

Already Sam and Lysta were being sick, and Seth, who always had a full belly, was getting ready to shift his lunch. I think we triggered one another off, a chain reaction, bending over bowls amid Calor gas canisters, wheelbarrows, bags of cement powder, a row of fridges, none of it looking particularly secure, held in place by a single strand of rope.

We were a sorrowful sight, all of us retching, battered by the roar of the engines. We couldn't even keep down a drink of water. Lysta kept trying to get the words out that she wanted to go home. I couldn't blame her; what a few days they had been through. But the storm blew itself out, and they all fell asleep, including Ros, heads on each other's shoulders, like a little group of puppets.

They were still asleep when we arrived in Aghios Kirikos, the main port of Ikaria, which rose up in a semicircle of multicoloured houses, their windows reflecting the cabin lights of the ferry that towered above the quayside.

All the noise of docking such a large boat went on around us: the engines louder than ever; the grinding of the winches as the great steel tailgate was slowly lowered on to the cobbled stones. With the manoeuvring complete and the hawsers tied around the bollards, the ferry gave out one last deafening blast that echoed in the hills.

As we disembarked, you'd have thought we had known the crew for years. Those despairing looks, as if they were saying goodbye to old friends; we embraced them all, including the chef, who gave us a bag of food. The captain shook my hand, saying, 'This is Ikaria. This is what you English call the rush hour, when a ship comes in. It doesn't get any busier than this in the winter.'

There to greet the ferry were half a dozen men in pick-up trucks, a mule pulling a trailer, and a policeman on a motorbike wearing sunglasses. He looked like a cop straight out of an American TV show.

On the far side of the town square were the inviting lights of a taverna. We were all hungry now, having recovered from our seasickness, and made our way there past a group of tethered donkeys who stood, with their eyes half closed, grinding their teeth.

The first thing I did was take out my phrase book. But before I could order anything, a hand was on my shoulder.

'It's all right, I can speak English. You have come from Piraeus and are tired and hungry.'

I nodded.

'Trust me, I will make you a delicious meal.'

'*Pos se lene?*' I said it in Greek, wanting to show off to Sam and Lysta.

'My name is Stamati.'

Probably in his late forties, he had thinning dark hair, a few days' growth of beard on a dimpled chin. A gold crucifix round his neck hung in enough chest hair to stuff a mattress.

'You speak very good English, Stamati.'

'Yes. My sister, she is married to an Englishman. I go once a year to Manchester, where they have a restaurant. It runs in the family.'

'I think we have just made our first friend on Ikaria,' I told the children. And he became a closer friend when he put on the table for each of them a teaspoon of vanilla paste in a glass of water.

'It is a traditional Greek drink that children love.'

And they did. It put them in the best mood since we had left Wales.

It was impossible to eat all that Stamati placed before us. A huge moussaka, a bottle of Samos wine, and *kataifi*, which looked like shredded wheat, the sweetest dessert that had ever passed my lips.

As we ate, the remains of an orange sun lit the fishing boats within the harbour walls. Lights suspended through the sycamore trees came on in the square. A church bell rang out and, as if summoned, people came from their houses in groups, some with smartly dressed children; others arrived on mopeds, to mingle with their friends. This social gathering is what happens on summer evenings in the Mediterranean and obviously continues in the winter.

After I'd paid Stamati sixty drachma, he sat down with us.

'Now what brings an English family with such young children to Ikaria on a cold February night?'

'I don't know. We got on the first boat leaving Piraeus.'

'And how long will you stay with us?'

'I'm not sure. Maybe many months, could be longer than that.'

I could tell by the astonishment on Stamati's face that he found this hard to believe. 'Where will you sleep tonight?'

'Do you know where we can find some rooms?'

'For how long?'

'I don't know. Maybe a few days.'

'I have a house here in Aghios Kirikos. It's small, but you're welcome to stay there.'

So ended four days on coach and boat: in Stamati's little whitewashed house, with its blue-painted windows overlooking the Aegean Sea where I stood and stared, while Ros and the children slept in two iron beds.

It was a good time to reassure myself that we had done the right thing, although getting here had been clumsy and uncomfortable. I suddenly allowed myself to feel exhausted. I didn't bother to get undressed, just fell into bed, all of us squeezed in next to each other. I wished I could have drifted off listening to some music. I had a portable cassette player in the suitcase; I'd find it tomorrow.

2

Finding Lefkada

The next day we had our first look around Aghios Kirikos. Despite the thin mattress and broken springs, we had all slept heavily, waking up much later than usual; a cold wind blowing in from the sea did little to revive us. Most of the shops were padlocked, no doubt closed until the summer came. Only the kiosk on the seafront, selling cigarettes and newspapers, was doing any business. In the cobbled back streets and alleyways there were a couple of greengrocers and a butcher, and the smell of newly baked bread coming from a bakery. We stood outside a dress shop with its stripped mannequins, Sam certain he could see their goose pimples.

But Stamati was always open and happy to cook us a meal, so we went to his restaurant for a late lunch. I looked at my family, thinking, what have I done, dragging them out here on a whim, uprooting their whole lives? I'd had this feeling before, coming over me like a black wave after we'd bought the farm in Wales, not knowing what I had let us all in for.

'Mum, have you noticed what's not here, but you would find in Penygroes?' asked Lysta, observant as ever about her surroundings.

'Let Sam guess,' said Ros.

'A fish and chip shop?' he suggested.

'Yes, you're right. Maybe they don't eat fish and chips here,' I said.

'That's not what I was thinking,' said Lysta. 'There are no traffic lights. And no zebra crossings either.'

This game continued as we looked across the harbour, which was crowded with little fishing boats. A donkey passed carrying a woman and child, the mother whipping the animal's backside with a stick.

'They must be late for school,' said Lysta. 'That poor donkey. He can't go any faster.'

'Dad, can I ask you something that I think is quite interesting?' said Sam.

'Fire away. What is it?'

'If we had donkeys in Wales would they have to stop at red lights?'

'I'll have to check the Highway Code, but they probably would.'

After a slow lunch of minestrone soup and fresh bread straight from the local bakery, the children enjoyed what was now their favourite, vanilla paste in a glass of water. Then Lysta had another bout of homesickness. Stamati brought her a piece of paper and she wrote her second letter home, not to her friend Eleri this time, but to her grandmother Dinah.

'What have you said to Granny?' I asked.

'Most of it's a secret so I can't tell you.'

'What part can you tell me?'

'That I don't know why we're here.'

'Yes,' said Sam. 'Why have we come all the way here, and it's not even warm and sunny?'

'Because we are on an adventure. You wait and see, lots of exciting things are going to happen,' I said. 'Aren't they, Ros?'

'Of course. We'll move into a lovely house and you'll make lots of new friends.'

'And get a television?' Lysta demanded.

'Yes, and watch *Tiswas* on Saturdays like we did at home,' agreed Sam.

'We've only been here a day. Give us a chance,' said Ros.

I told them that after lunch everyone on the island had a siesta. 'It's an old custom. Children are not allowed to talk for an hour.'

'It's impossible not to talk for an hour if you're awake,' said Sam, certain he was correct.

'Why don't you try it this afternoon? I'll give you twenty pence each if you manage it.' Attempting bribery was something I often did.

'But we can't spend English money here,' said Sam.

'Well, I'll give you twenty drachma.'

Ros thought they would never let us have an hour's sleep, but they did, and we all slept, and when we woke again the sun had already gone down behind the mountains. In the twilight we walked a little way out of town and gazed at the sea. We were still acclimatising, not feeling sociable, ending up in Stamati's for a third time. He must have loved us; as far as I could tell we were his only customers wanting food. The others were just drinking coffee or ouzo.

Yet all he wanted to do was ask about our life in North Wales. He hadn't bothered to take our order before he sat down with us.

'I want to tell my mother all about where you come from. She loves to hear about faraway places; she has never left Ikaria.'

'Well, where do I begin?' I said. 'There are so many stories.' Before I could get another word out, Sam and Lysta took over, telling Stamati that I spent most of my time chasing pigs and looking for sheep that had strayed.

'Yes, and once Dad had to catch a pig that had run into a shop in Caernarfon.' It was one of the many incidents that they loved to talk about.

All the while Stamati sat as if engrossed, but I doubted he understood everything he was hearing. It made us sound like a family living from one mishap to the next.

'We're not usually like this,' I said. 'In fact, we're very sensible and well balanced.'

'You were a farmer. Yes, I can see that, with your broad shoulders.' Which he sank his fingers into, causing Ros to raise her eyebrows and give me a wry smile.

In the evening the people sitting under the sycamore trees in the main square seemed bemused by our presence, giving us quizzical looks which gave way to warm smiles for the children. A huddle of grandmothers, all wearing head scarves, beckoned to us. We weren't used to all this attention, but it was the children they were drawn to, stretching out their arms, almost pleading with us to join them.

'Let's go and introduce ourselves,' said Ros.

I got out my phrase book and in a few minutes they knew all our names and that we had come from Wales. From what I could gather, we were the first Welsh people to have visited the island. It caused confusion trying to explain that Ros was Welsh and I was English; I gave up any idea of telling them that our children were half English and half Welsh. But everything I said was met by a row of smiling, nodding heads as if they had understood every word.

'Leesta, Saam, Sarth.' It was close enough, so it was my turn to nod my head. One by one they disappeared and returned with treats: something that looked like Turkish delight, little sachets of coated almonds, cherries dipped in a thick syrup. Sam, Lysta and Seth tried them all, and at about ten o'clock, when normally they would have been ready for sleep, they had the energy to run around the square. Ikarian children didn't seem to have a bedtime, even when they had to go to school in the morning.

'Why are the cats so thin, Mum?' asked Lysta, as we eventually walked back to Stamati's house and to bed.

'I suppose because no one feeds them.'

'It's cruel; they're starving.'

On the second day we woke early. Only Stamati was up,

sweeping the pavement in front of his restaurant. There was no one else about, just a stray dog, a few pigeons under the café tables and two donkeys parked outside a hairdresser's, staring at the photographs of coiffured women.

At last we all felt wide awake. Sam and Lysta skipped along, Seth running behind them, Ros with a brightness back in her face, smiling, her wild, frizzy hair buffeted in the gusts of wind. She had packed a picnic of sorts: not sandwiches, but food from the chef on the ferry, leftovers from Stamati's generous portions, and sweets from the friendly grannies in the square.

For the first time we had the energy to explore. We climbed the hills above Aghios Kirikos and looked out over the Aegean, vast and empty without a vessel to be seen, the distant shape of the island of Fourni like a spined dinosaur sleeping in a deep blue sea.

That morning we walked for over an hour and saw no one, passing only half-built houses perched on the steep slopes. Who were they waiting for, these deserted dwellings that seemed abandoned even before being completed? It was only as we were returning that we met an old peasant pushing his bike, the carcass of a goat strapped around his back. Such had been the effort of his climb he could not even raise a smile. I told Ros the place seemed quieter than a ghost town; even the ghosts had left.

'Maybe we should see if we can find an island with a bit more life,' she suggested.

'No, it's too soon. Let's give it a month.'

That night in the Casino café, where the locals were playing backgammon – *tavli* as they called it – an old priest who had been sitting with them came over to us. I was about to try my first glass of ouzo; it was cold and getting colder, and I needed to warm myself up. Ros was trying a Metaxa brandy.

He spoke English and knew exactly who we were.

'It will snow tomorrow. I have some blankets I can bring you,' he said in the benevolent voice that seemed to go with his calling.

'The children need to be warm. It is not right for you to be in Stamati's house. It is for summer, not now, the middle of winter.'

And sure enough, in the morning the snow was falling, not the large wind-driven flakes of Wales but much more gentle than that, lightly covering the main square. The winter sun was trying to break through the snow-filled clouds. It snowed on the fishing boats and out into the sea, which was not a sight I had expected to see on a Greek island.

Father Antonis brought us blankets and, although he didn't say it, I could tell he couldn't understand why we were here. He was forever stroking the children's heads, no doubt pitying them for having such irresponsible parents.

A week later we moved. It was one of those chance meetings: we were exploring the island, hitching on the coastal road, even though cars were few and far between. Sam and Lysta continuously held out their thumbs, despite my telling them it was only necessary when we could hear a vehicle coming. I think they persisted because they thought it would magically make one appear. We had walked at least a couple of miles, Seth sitting on my shoulders picking at my hair like a baby gorilla searching for fleas.

An out-of-control old Renault swerved to avoid us and stopped just a few feet from the edge, narrowly avoiding crashing on to the rocks below. One of its tyres had exploded.

The driver did not emerge, and when I knocked on his window to check whether he was injured I could see that he was, but not from the incident we had just witnessed. His right arm was in a sling; it made me wonder how he could have been driving in the first place. I opened the door and helped him out. He had that look I was getting used to: unkempt, stubble not far from being a beard. It appeared Ikarian men fell out of bed and straight into their clothes. Dishevelment was definitely the fashion.

When he saw the shreds of rubber strewn across the road, he exhaled a lot of Greek bad language into the morning air. After fumbling in his jacket for a cigarette, he sat on a boulder smoking, taking long deep drags, completely ignoring us. With his arm in a sling, dealing with the tyre was beyond him, so that's when I stepped in. After getting the spare from the boot, I jacked up the car and changed the wheel. Even Ros was impressed by how I had taken charge.

'It's nothing,' I said nonchalantly. 'God, how many times did I do that on the farm?'

'Dad, don't forget you couldn't change the tyre on my Tonka truck once,' said Sam. I remembered that toy of his, the one he used to fill with earth and push up and down the drive.

But we'd made Dimitri a happy man, and after we got talking I told him we were looking for somewhere to live that had views across the sea and wasn't too far from Aghios Kirikos. He said his brother owned a house nearby at Lefkada, so we walked on while he went ahead in the car, the Renault 4 too small to carry us all. Besides, I didn't want to put our lives at risk being driven by a one-armed driver in what was no more than a tin can. From what I could gather, he had broken his arm when his donkey had reared up while he was strapping a fridge on its back. It was a bit confusing, but I think a ferry had blasted its horn and terrified the poor beast.

After fifteen minutes or so, several houses came into view. This had to be Lefkada, for I could see Dimitri's car parked outside a small, single-storey house. He showed us around it, two rooms with two front doors, so you had to leave by one door to enter the other bedroom. We didn't really like it, but we would have some privacy and it was quiet, unlike Stamati's place where through the walls you could hear people going to the lavatory. It certainly had lovely views over the Aegean. There was no bathroom; we had to do the business in a hole in the ground, some twenty yards behind the house. Ros grimaced at the thought.

'Look, we didn't come here expecting a five-star hotel.' That didn't go down too well.

'I doubt very much this would get one star,' she retorted.

We took it because it was cheap: a hundred drachma (around £1.50) a week.

Dimitri helped us out by putting three beds for the children in one room, and Ros and I had a double in the other. It was a real luxury for us to be sleeping in our own bed again, and far better to be here than in Aghios Kirikos. We were given too much attention there; we needed to be alone as a family.

There was no electricity, just a Calor gas stove in the kitchen area which began three feet from our bed. The most annoying thing was the cold water tap that dripped into a cracked basin. Every night I had to stick a sock up it, to stop it getting on Ros's nerves. We had candles and plenty of blankets; I was sure we could survive here until the warmer weather came.

Dimitri visited only once to see how we were settling in. I gave him a month's rent in advance, and then he was off to Athens where he sold olive oil to the smart hotels. From then on I was to give the rent to his ageing mother who lived on the waterfront in Therma, a village the other side of Aghios Kirikos. We would see him again in July when the weather, as he put it, would be '*poli zesti*', very hot.

What a transformation had taken place. It was quite remarkable how quickly the children adapted to their sparse surroundings. In the candlelight, they were happy to play a game of shadow-dancing, creating creatures that pranced about on the walls above their beds. Not once, despite their earlier moaning, did they complain about not having a television. Nor did they demand toys or sweets when we went shopping. They expected nothing and seemed content to draw, or invent their own games to play outside the house.

As for me, I felt we had arrived, that the holiday was over. I was ready to look for work and it was time for Ros to start teaching the children. It was March and our third week here. I wished the spring would hurry up and we could feel a bit of warmth in the wind. Not that this was anything like the harsh winters in North Wales, but at least at home I could smoke a joint in front of a roaring log fire and watch *Match of the Day* on a Saturday night. I didn't tell Ros that was the only thing I missed, though it was a question I knew would come up one day.

I had a coffee with Stamati; I wanted to thank him again for all his help when we first arrived and also to find out whether he had the answer to something on my mind. Ever since we'd been here I'd felt drawn to the sea; I wanted to be a fisherman, out on the Aegean under a huge sky. I asked him if he knew anyone who needed help on their boat. He did, of course, 'but you are so thin, you will be blown overboard. Then what will your wife say? She will blame me for becoming a widow.'

'I need to work. I need to make some money,' I said.

'There is little work to be found here in the winter,' said Stamati. 'But I have liked you since that first day, and I will help you.'

He said this with a look in his eyes I wasn't sure about. Was there a price I was going to have to pay? For a while he stirred his Nescafé in gentle circles; I could see things fizzing through his mind.

'Wait, I will return.' And he disappeared, leaving me sitting there, staring down at my worn-out shoes. Something else we would have to buy, unless I could glue the sole to the upper, but footwear didn't last long walking up and down the coast road to Lefkada.

Across the main square I could see the Poste Restante where we collected our occasional mail and posted our letters, mostly from Lysta to her school friends. She had sent at least half a dozen to Eleri and received not a single reply, which had upset her deeply. It only took a week for a letter to get back to the United Kingdom, so surely she should have heard back by now. But it was always Lysta who went to see if there was any post and returned disappointed. I knew our PO Box was 57 and, as there was no sign of Stamati, I went and enquired for myself.

I walked back to the café clutching a handful of letters, all but one in Eleri's handwriting. I didn't know why Lysta had never been given the post; maybe she had simply been misunderstood. I opened the other letter; it was from my mother, five pages of news from England, including a cutting from the sports page with the latest football results. She told me Jack was still a shepherd, and that he and Corinna were enjoying life in Gloucestershire. Meg, his old sheepdog, had retired and Moss, my border collie, was now his number one worker. As soon as I read that I could see Moss sweeping in a large circle, gathering up the flock. The letter ended with the hope I was taking all the necessary precautions.

Stamati eventually returned, bringing with him a wild-eyed young man called Stelios, who looked as if he had just walked out of the sea. His thick hair seemed fixed in permanent little waves that rolled across his head in a north-westerly direction. His hands, when we shook, were rougher than a hill farmer's, coarse, the skin dry and cracked. I took to him immediately, he had a dishevelled tiredness I felt at home with. He was another one with several days' growth. Deeply tanned from years of sun and sea, he could not have turned thirty; his eyebrows were bleached and sparkled with salt crystals above two exhausted eyes. He had enough English, spoken in a gruff voice that came from smoking or shouting into the wind. He leant back and eyed me up. 'You are sure, yes? You have the strength for this work?'

'Yes, I am sure. I was a farmer. I can carry a pig over my shoulders.'

'It is not the same as pulling in the nets. Shake my hand again.'

I did, gripping it tightly.

'All right, that is good.'

'When do we start, and how much will you pay me?'

'You are a man in a hurry,' he said. 'I give you five hundred drachma a day' – he didn't wait for an answer – 'but first we must fish together. I never fish with a man I do not know. It's lonely out there, even lonelier if you don't like each other.'

So a couple of days later we went out into the Aegean in his boat *Panagia*, Mother of God. About thirty foot long, painted blue and orange, it had a small, cluttered cabin I could hardly stand up in, with two cramped berths on either side. Beneath a hatch on the deck was the engine, which bore an oval plaque embossed with the words *Made by Listers of Derby*.

I sat at the bow as we made our way out of the harbour. The sea, a glassy blue, reflected the winter sun as the coastline gradually disappeared behind us. A flock of birds whizzed past, their wingtips no more than a foot above the water. The cold Aegean breeze whistled in my ears. There was a freshness to the air that I found exhilarating, and I took deep breaths as if I were drinking it.

After he'd cast his nets, Stelios came and joined me, letting the boat drift. He told me about his life as an Ikarian fisherman and I told him about my life in North Wales as a farmer. Our two lives, I said, shared a common thread: the weather. I wasn't sure he understood me; it made me realise how complicated the English language can be. I needed to choose my words more carefully. I told him how I had lost sheep buried in a snowstorm, while he recalled the night with his father when gale force winds blew their boat onto rocks and smashed the rudder. They had drifted for hours before being towed back to Aghios Kirikos.

Any doubts he might have had about me must have vanished, for he simply said 'Do we like each other?' and, smiling, turned the boat back to shore. And so, having made my living from the land, I would now earn it from the sea. Gazing out across the waves at the shoreline of Ikaria, I felt a curious sense that I was returning to something in the past, perhaps of a life I'd already lived.

After we had secured the boat we sat at the end of the quayside, Stelios smoking a Karelia, a Greek cigarette with a curious, musty smell. He wanted to close the deal, just like the hill farmers, who never dragged things out, and we sealed it with a spit into the hand.

'We fish two days a week, five hundred drachma a day. I give you some fish, maybe octopus, squid, sometimes barbunia. Are you happy with this?'

I was, but I wasn't so sure Ros would be.

꒕

I suppose the taverna at Lefkada was what you would call our local, since we lived less than a hundred yards away. It was run by a married couple, Yannis and Maria, who had been born in the same mountain village and must have been in their seventies. 'Taverna' was probably too grand a title for the place: a dozen or so tables with rush-seated chairs on the bare earth surrounded by eucalyptus trees. At the top of a short flight of steps behind this area was a low building with a flaky green door and shuttered windows hiding two rooms that Maria let out to the occasional game tourist, if they didn't mind sharing with the cheeses that hung from the beams. In each room were a couple of old cast-iron beds with mattresses so thin you could roll them up.

The building that housed a small kitchen looked like a converted cowshed made from breeze blocks. It had a corrugated roof and, like everything else, was whitewashed: the tree trunks, a row of olive oil tins used as flowerpots, the low stone wall that separated the tables from the coastal road, even an old wheelbarrow that reflected the winter sun, had all seen the paintbrush.

It was a very basic set-up. One day when I was walking past I saw Maria hosing down the plates people had just eaten from and cleaning them with a worn down scrubbing brush. There were more bristles on her husband's chin.

She and Yannis, I'm sure, barely covered their costs, probably making just enough money in the summer to keep them going through the winter months. She didn't have the strength to lift the pile of plates she had just washed, and Yannis made several journeys to carry them back to the kitchen.

Little did I know then what a pivotal part the taverna would play in our lives as the social centre of our tiny universe, where we would spend our evenings chatting to visitors, finding out where they'd come from and where they were heading. Most just turned up, dropped their rucksacks for a while and moved on, but a few stayed and we got to know them well, talking long into the night under the star-filled skies.

It was here that I gradually acquired a taste for retsina, despite its unfortunate hint of pine disinfectant that lingers in the mouth as if you are drinking lavatory cleaner. Ros wouldn't go near it, and if you wanted to indulge you couldn't get it by the glass, only in small bottles. But it was a cheap way to get pissed, although it did odd things to your stomach.

I'd just finished my third glass when I said to Ros, 'You know, this stuff plays around with your head. I thought I just saw a nun go past on a moped.'

'You did, and she wasn't hanging around,' as a cloud of dust engulfed the taverna.

'Don't tell me she was being chased by Henry VIII on a Harley-Davidson.'

'I didn't think retsina was a hallucinogenic.'

'You know, it doesn't taste that bad, once your mouth is anaesthetised.'

'Dad's not making sense again,' Lysta butted in.

'What do you mean, again?'

The conversation changed direction, a full one hundred and eighty degrees.

'What's going to happen out at sea if you and Stelios get stuck into the retsina? Can you drink and steer a boat?' asked Ros.

'Well, it's not like driving a car, is it?' I said. 'Anyway, I have no idea if Stelios has a drink when he's fishing.'

I could tell Ros was anxious, and her tone didn't lighten up.

'You promise you'll wear a life jacket? You know you're accident prone.'

'I really don't know what has given you that impression.'

'Well, I don't think I was imagining it when you nearly cut your foot off with that chainsaw, for instance. Or when you had to be rescued from the sea at Dinas Dinlle. Don't you remember the undertow from those gigantic waves that kept dragging you back?'

'All right,' I conceded. 'There has been the odd occasion when I've got into dodgy situations. But that was then. I'm not going to make a habit of it.'

I knew she was right. I had nearly injured myself on the farm several times for no other reason than a lack of self-awareness. I cheered her up by painting a picture of me coming home with the fish I had caught out in the Aegean, bringing them to her with the smell of sea salt in my hair, hugging her in the twilight, laying out on the table the fresh squid that we would eat by candlelight.

'All very romantic, wouldn't you agree, Ros?'

Well she did, not that she admitted it, but she looked a bit dreamy, with the flicker of a smile.

'I'm worried for you, that's all.'

3

Out on the Aegean

The children's first day at school. We'd called it Lefkada School to give it a proper name. Ros explained to me the psychological bridge the children had to cross, from her as their mother to her as their teacher, otherwise it wouldn't work. We had an assortment of books from Carmel primary school and the curriculum for the year ahead. It was important to both of us, and Ros wanted to create an atmosphere that would set the tone. Until the warmer weather arrived, our bedroom would be the classroom. After breakfast, we turned the bed sideways to make space for the two chairs Maria had given us and our kitchen table became a school desk.

'It's what they need,' she said. 'To have a routine, some structure and discipline back in their lives. Will you tell them they need to be clean and tidy for school?' Ros said, anxious not to be the only disciplinarian.

Sam and Lysta were quite excited by it all, while Seth was oblivious, chasing a fly that was buzzing around the room. I suggested I should take him for the morning, that he would disrupt the class. But Ros said he would be all right lying on the floor drawing and, besides, she wanted him to be a part of it.

Suddenly I had time on my hands. Ros had said the night before that she'd be uncomfortable with me watching her playing her schoolteacher role. I reminded her that most of life was role-playing, particularly in a marriage, keeping things spiced up, wink, wink. She threw a shoe at me.

So I took myself off, heading to Xylosirtis, a small village some five kilometres along the coast road from Lefkada. It felt strange to be out walking on my own, not having to wait for children to catch up, back to my natural brisk pace. And not engaged in conversation, silent, the way it used to be walking in the fields at Dyffryn, only now I didn't have Moss, my dog, at my side.

When I reached Xylosirtis I found a quiet village of no more than a few whitewashed houses in the morning sunlight. I thought I would walk straight through it without meeting a soul, until I saw a solemn figure with a heavy tread walking towards me beside a donkey carrying two cages full of chickens on its back. Tied around his head was a black scarf and he had a thick grey beard so overgrown that it was hard to imagine how he had lit the cigarette now long finished, that hung from his lips. Surely not something to be tried when the wind was blowing. If he hadn't stopped at the taverna we would have passed each other. He cast a furtive glance at me, throwing a handful of carob on the ground and tethering the donkey to a lemon tree. I'm not one for guessing a person's age, but he was getting on. He bent over his coffee, lifting the cup no more than a few inches to reach his mouth. I'd forgotten my phrase book, so started with what little Greek I knew.

'*Kali mera*,' followed by '*pos se lene*?' Good morning, what is your name?

'Stephanos,' he said. And so began a conversation that took me on a journey into an old man's life. We sat for over an hour and the only person we saw was his niece, Taviva. She appeared on her bicycle and stayed, translating the adventures of this Cretan who fought in the resistance during the Second World War.

He took faded photographs of a group of young men from his wallet, all killed by the Nazis. He blew little kisses into the air, and then surprisingly started to sing 'We'll Meet Again'. He looked at me with a pair of sad eyes, speaking his only English.

'Vera Lynn, good.'

I asked Taviva if he was a contented man, and she put it to him. As he got up from his chair he smiled, giving his reply to his niece.

'He's just a communist now,' she said.

🔳

According to Ros's luminous wristwatch, I had woken up two hours before I needed to. I always did when I had to be somewhere early. The shuttered light had not slanted through our window yet. So I lay in bed remembering the last time I had worked for someone, which must have been at least eight years ago, in a sausage-skin warehouse, of all places, in the east end of London.

No wonder it felt like my first day on the job, because that's exactly what it was, going fishing with Stelios. It wasn't going to sea that worried me, but a niggling doubt about my sea legs if it got rough. I didn't want to spend my first morning vomiting over the side of the boat. After what we had gone through on the ferry, I decided not to eat before I left. If there's nothing in the stomach, then there's nothing to come up. Ros had reminded me the night before that red was for starboard, green for port. As it happens I'm colour blind, but I was sure port and starboard didn't come into a Greek fisherman's life. She was also concerned that I had no knowledge of knots and asked me what a sheepshank was. I said it was a joint of meat you cooked in a slow oven. All she was doing was expressing her fears, but I thought it was necessary to mention that I couldn't tie my shoelaces until I was ten.

Ros didn't understand how much the idea of being a fisherman out in the Aegean excited me. She was afraid some disaster would occur and I'd be lost at sea. I hadn't told her that Stelios had said we would sometimes be night fishing off the island of Samos.

I left without kissing her, not wanting to wake her up. Allowing myself half an hour to walk to the harbour, I stepped out into the still air of the night, before dawn glimmered on the horizon. I hadn't yet seen the sun come up over Ikaria, but as I walked and the earth turned, the distant shapes of islands slowly emerged from the gloom, Fourni and Samos becoming visible, defined in a soft, pinkish light. The flowing sunrise washed over the sea, and all that had been of the night gradually disappeared.

Stelios had a younger brother, Theo, who usually fished with him, but recently had got distracted by girls and become unreliable. There was a big gap in their ages, nearly eleven years. Theo was only eighteen and Stelios said he was irresponsible, whereas he could depend on someone like me with mouths to feed. He understood the weight a married man carried, being the breadwinner. He had a wife and two children and also supported not only his mother and father but his grandparents as well; they all depended on him. There were no social benefits handed out in Greece; no wonder he was fed up with Theo, pulling girls instead of his weight.

From the road I could see Stelios busy on his boat, working on the nets. It was cold but the sea was flat, and I was relieved to see only the tiniest waves making it to the shore, no more than ripples. Seabirds with yellow beaks floated in the clear water and I could see shoals of silver fish swimming close to the surface. A semicircle of orange buoys broke the view between the harbour walls and the white sails of a lone yacht.

He greeted me warmly, heating up coffee in the cabin, wearing a faded Kansas USA baseball cap, a cigarette hanging from the corner of his mouth.

'You're not dressed for fishing,' he said, throwing me an oilskin coat and a pair of cut down wellingtons.

'Today I show you how a fisherman makes his living.'

He laughed, winding a coil of rope neatly around his forearm. 'We will soon see what you are made of, yes?'

There were piles of nets and floats all along one side of the boat, worn car tyres every few feet. I constantly had to watch where I was walking, since everything seemed to be a potential hazard.

He turned on the engine and cast off, I think is the expression – we certainly didn't set sail, because we didn't have any – and headed out to sea, leaving behind the harbour walls and lighthouse of Aghios Kirikos. The engine spluttered in the bowels of the boat, a throaty sound you would hear from a car with a broken exhaust, clouds of blue smoke billowing out behind us.

At the stern Stelios held the tiller, puffing on his cigarette, staring into the distance, his collar up against the wind. I stood at the bow, the deck hand on his maiden voyage, feeling the rhythm of the boat gently rising and falling, the air biting my cheeks, smelling the diesel fumes. I didn't feel seasick at all and why should I, with the sea so flat and calm? All around us was nothing but the great blue expanse of the Aegean, empty but for our little vessel chugging along under a huge sky. Where we were heading I had no idea. Stelios obviously knew, not that I had seen him go into the cabin to check the compass. No stars above to guide us, just a blood-red sun rising.

After what felt like about an hour he reduced the revs of the engine and suddenly sprang into action unwinding the nets, feeding them through a steel spool. They trailed out into the sea and slowly sank, leaving only the floats visible. Seagulls appeared from nowhere, a noisy army of them circling the boat.

'Why here?' I asked him, my first words for some time. 'Why put the nets down here?'

'Why not here?' as if it was obvious. 'You know what instinct is?'

I nodded. 'Of course.'

'Well then, you know why here.'

'No electronic equipment to help you?'

'Ha! I live the sea, I feel the sea, and my father before me, you understand?'

That was my first lesson in the art of fishing, that there was no science to it, that for Stelios it was all about intuition. And it appealed to me because it came from the man. It was all so simple, as long as his inner faculties didn't let him down.

Once the nets were cast we headed to a small cove and dropped anchor. A swell rocked the boat. Stelios brought out a basket of bread, tomatoes and onions from the cabin. There were no plates, we didn't need them, just a wooden tray, two glasses and a bottle of retsina. We sat and ate beneath the stony cliffs, the water breaking over the exposed rocks. The winter sun gave out a gentle warmth as I chewed on a few mouthfuls of bread, sipping a glass of retsina. I didn't want to be seasick and refused when he passed me the bottle.

'*Ochi*,' I said. No.

'No sea legs yet, heh?' he said with a little self-contained laugh. He told me it reminded him of how the previous year six tourists had hired him for the day to take them to a hidden beach.

'Nudists,' he said, 'from Frankfurt. The Germans, they like to take off their clothes, and play silly games. Ha! you should watch them having fun, playing what they call naked volley ball, all their stuff, you know, swinging around, and then they drink, yes, and are sick all over the boat.'

He laughed again, offering me the bottle. 'I tell no one if you are sick.' But I still declined and left him to finish it.

Then he turned on a transistor, putting it on the cabin roof, and tuning in to a music station. Whether because of the retsina or just for his love of the song, he sang extravagantly, 'Pende pano, pende cato,' strumming an imaginary bouzouki.

'Now you sing!' So I did, the easy bit, *Pende pano, pende cato*.

He slapped me on the back. 'Bravo. You can sing, my friend!'

The water was becoming choppy. For the first time in what had been a calm clear day, cloud formations were appearing from the horizon, rolling upwards and claiming the whole sky, subduing the light to an overcast greyness. Things can happen quickly at sea, when the weather suddenly changes, and you realise how vulnerable you are to the power of nature.

Stelios showed a different side of himself; instantly the song-and-dance man had disappeared. We set off rapidly, the engine straining, going full throttle into a headwind. The waves broke over the bow, soaking me, ahead of us nothing but the great swell of the sea. The boat thumped as it rose and fell.

It amused me to see that somehow he had lit a cigarette in the howling wind. Surely he couldn't inhale a single drag of it. He shouted to me to put on my oilskin, no easy task when you're being thrown about the place. There was no rhythm to it, just a continual battering of the senses, as if I was being beaten up by the elements. It made me feel alive in a way I had never felt before.

When I saw the white polystyrene floats ahead, I shouted to Stelios several times, but my voice didn't reach him so I waved instead, throwing my arms around to show him I could see them. In acknowledgement, he raised his head slightly and dropped the revs, until we were close enough to hook the nets. He seemed to have forgotten I was English and spoke to me in Greek, moving about the boat in a hurry. Maybe he thought I was Theo.

Then he turned on the hydraulic spool and began hauling in the nets, hand over hand, pulling them on board and dropping them on to the deck. I leant over the bow watching the catch coming up from the deep, hearing the continual sound of water slapping the side of the boat as fish of all sizes passed beside me. And then as quickly as it had blown up the wind eased, and in the distance I could see blue sky breaking through the cloud.

Stelios handed me two plastic buckets, one for squid, the other for octopus. That was where the money was, the fisherman's prize. I was to yell at him when I saw one; I was so involved in what I was doing I suddenly realised I hadn't felt seasick at all.

It was an eerie sight, my first octopus with its two staring eyes, like something dragged up from a dark dream. I knew I had to pull the slimy creature from the net; it would slip through my fingers if I was squeamish. I shivered at the thought that it would cling to my skin, its tentacles entwined around my arm. I shouted to Stelios and he came quickly to show me what had to be done. He grabbed it aggressively with one hand as it clung to the other, putting up a fight, refusing to be pulled free. Then he hurled it on to the deck, not once but twice, to make sure it was dead, and dropped it into the bucket.

'They can fool you, pretending to be dead,' Stelios said. 'Kill them quickly, otherwise they will slip away and jump back into the sea. They are worth many drachma, you understand.'

For the next few minutes we worked in silence, me watching every fold of the net, moving forward to pull out the fish, throwing them unsorted into plastic boxes that slid around behind me. Amongst the many that were hauled up from the deep I recognised red mullet – which Stelios called barbunia – mackerel and sardines. Stelios worked at a furious rate, never tiring, sea spray dripping from his forehead. It was the longest I'd seen him without a cigarette in his mouth.

Suddenly he pushed me aside with both hands as I was about to grab a particularly ugly fish with a large spiny head and a huge mouth.

'Not this one! You understand? Poisonous!' And with a knife he raised up the spines along its back. 'You see this? Here is the poison, in the tips.'

He told me it was a scorpion fish and could put you in hospital, indeed had killed many people. He carefully picked it up by its tail fin and hurled it back into the sea, shouting, '*Ai sto dialo!*' Go to the devil.

'You remember this fish, my friend. It could take your life.'

There was no time to dwell upon my own mortality as the nets continued to come up and more octopus appeared. Luckily Stelios didn't see the one that climbed out of the bucket and slipped away to escape over the side. A part of me was glad that it had made it back into the darkness below. We had also caught several squid, and some rather strange-looking crabs that crawled around the deck until I threw them back into the water. I could only think that the reason Stelios showed no interest in them was because they were inedible and therefore not worth anything.

On the journey back, he gave me one of Theo's pullovers; he could see I was freezing. For a while I lost control of my jaw, my teeth literally chattering. I wanted to be back with Ros and the children. It felt as if we'd been out at sea for a long time. The sun was low in the sky when we finally reached Aghios Kirikos.

After securing either end of the boat to the bollards, we lifted the catch on to the harbour side. I was exhausted with a fatigue I hadn't experienced before. Still swaying with the rhythm of the sea, I sat with my back against the wall, staring blankly. I asked Stelios if he was happy with the day; what I really wanted to hear was that he was happy with me. He smiled, giving me a bag of fish.

'Here you are, my friend,' he said, patting me on the back.

'We survived the storm, Stelios . . . on my first day at sea.'

'My friend, that was no storm . . . it was what you English I think call a squall.'

Then his roaring laugh followed me as I made my way around the harbour wall, walking like a drunkard, my legs operating under a law of their own. It took a lot longer than usual to get back to Lefkada and by the time I returned home the day was dispersing its last colours, the mountain ridges alight with all the hues of twilight.

Through the night with Ros by my side I was still at sea, rising and falling with the waves, pulling octopus from a dripping net.

There were taxis in Aghios Kirikos, which were only ever on the move when a ferry docked, and there were a few buses, all of them parked up for the winter, covered in bird droppings. So if you wanted to get around, you had to stand out in the road and whoever was passing would stop and give you a lift. The children were definitely an asset; no one ever drove past us. Once a builder in his pick-up carried his mother from the cab and dumped her in the back with a goat and a bale of hay so that Ros and the children could travel up front. Ros was not happy at all to see the old woman manhandled from her seat, but she cheerfully waved our objections away.

It was a social occasion to go into a shop and buy the most trivial of things, like pencils for the children. The whole family would suddenly emerge from the back and we would be stuck there for twenty minutes while they caressed the children and patted their heads. I think they just loved being in our company.

The islanders never ceased to surprise us. Sometimes in the mornings we would find food left on the doorstep; loaves of bread, yoghurt and vegetables. Our neighbours must have tiptoed up during the night to leave these anonymous gifts, not seeking recognition for their kind acts. One day at the taverna we told Maria about it, but she shrugged her shoulders, obviously thinking it wasn't worth mentioning. Clearly, this generous hospitality was in their nature and didn't need to be talked about. She was more interested in showing Ros how to make spinach and feta pies, while Yannis hung a swing from a eucalyptus tree and played with the children.

It gave me a chance to go and get out my portable tape player and lie on the bed and listen to *Goats Head Soup* by the Rolling Stones. I had brought all my favourite tapes with me: Bob Marley, Pink Floyd, Cat Stevens, Neil Young. As I jumped from track to track, each song reminded me of Dyffryn. It seemed so long ago, but it had been only a few weeks since we'd left. When Lysta came and lay down next to me, she whispered in my ear that she only felt it once a day now, when she was going to sleep.

'Felt what?' I asked.

'That I want to go home.'

'So you like Ikaria now, do you?'

'I miss my friends and having a bicycle.'

'I have an idea,' I said. 'Do you have Eleri's phone number?'

'I think Mum's got it in her address book.'

'Well, we'll book a phone call to her. That will make you happy, won't it?'

We couldn't really afford it; we were getting low on money. I was determined not to ring my brother Jack, who had banked all the money from the sale of Dyffryn. It was going to have to buy us a house somewhere, some day; all I knew was that it was tied up in a deposit account, for how long I had no idea.

4

Datsun Jim and
Sister Ulita

Datsun Jim skidded to a dusty halt outside the taverna with a cement mixer in the back of his battered pick-up. He was half an hour late, but he didn't care about being on time. No one did, come to that. Maybe there wasn't a Greek word for punctuality. Or was it just on Ikaria that you turned up when it suited you? Being on time was unimportant, so what was the point of making an arrangement to meet anyone? Everything was *avrio*, tomorrow, which explained why there was no urgency about getting anything done. In England, the whole country would grind to a standstill, while here everything gradually ground to a start. Having to live with this total disregard for time put me in a bad mood. Ros said I would be better off just coming to terms with it, but she wasn't the one sitting around waiting.

It was probably why dotted about the landscape were half-finished breeze-block houses that hadn't had a day's work done on them since we'd arrived. Which was six weeks ago now, and I needed to be earning more money. Although I was still fishing with Stelios, we were down to our last two hundred pounds. So the offer of work from Datsun Jim (whose real name was Dimitrios; Sam had come up with the nickname, and it had stuck) had been good timing.

'*Kali mera*,' was all he said now, clearing empty cans of Coke and packets of cigarettes from the front seat. He was building a house for his brother, who lived in Detroit and was coming back to Ikaria in the summer. I knew it would never be finished by then. He only worked in the mornings, laying bricks while I mixed the cement. I asked him if he knew exactly when his brother was arriving and he gave me the Greek response that I now knew well: eyebrows raised and eyes half closed, he threw his head back and muttered, '*Ochi*.'

Whenever it was going to be, he carried on as always, stopping every twenty minutes to stare out across the sea, lost in some distant dream-world, until he broke this trance-like state by reaching for another can of Coke. He frequently wiped his face with a dirty handkerchief, into which he then blew his nose.

He was not old, no more than early forties, with thick dark hair up front and a bald patch behind. He carried around a bloated belly from all the Coke he drank, and was accompanied by a mongrel dog that he tied to a fig tree and sprayed every half an hour with insect repellent, because it was forever scratching itself. On my first day working with him, he showed me a girlie magazine.

'Yes, you like too?'

Sometimes he put a portable radio on the bonnet of the pick-up and, like Stelios, tuned it until he found some traditional Greek music, then lit a cigarette and started dancing, beckoning me to join him, which I felt I had to. With our hands on each other's shoulders, bending our knees, we danced around the pile of cement as it hardened in front of us. Often when he was bricklaying he would stop and talk about his brother Giorgos, his hero figure. One day he'd just been boasting about the big bucks Giorgos made working on the Cadillac assembly line when a friend of his turned up, walking beside a grey donkey loaded with six bags of cement which the two of them set about unloading. The mixer was still half full and if they didn't hurry up the contents would harden in no time. But neither of them moved with any urgency, lost in deep conversation, until I tapped Jim on the shoulder to make him aware of what was happening.

So he tipped the lot out of the mixer on to the ground, not bothered at all, and continued talking. That was when I knew the house would never be finished. After ten minutes he signalled to me to get into the back of the pick-up. His friend, an old timer, tied his donkey to an olive tree and got into the front seat, and we drove off. Was that it for the day? Where were we going and when were we coming back? I could see them laughing in the cab, Jim's friend looking at the girlie magazine, holding it up so I could see too.

They dropped me at the beach near Lefkada. Jim leant out of the window, shouted, 'No money. *Avrio*,' and drove off.

I hadn't even worked half a day and Ros would still be teaching the children. I was at a loose end, so I walked into the sea fully clothed with my sandals on, ghostly grey in my covering of cement powder, and floated on my back, my arms and legs outstretched like a starfish.

Datsun Jim had said he would pay me three hundred drachma a day. I should have asked for at least four hundred, but had thought that if he saw how hard I worked I could ask for more in a couple of weeks. But I realised now that that would never happen and I didn't know how much longer I could work with him. His lack of purpose or interest in getting the job done was frustrating. I liked to set myself a target and feel that sense of achievement one gets from a good day's work. And I was determined to survive out here and not resort to getting money wired over from England.

I'd sent my first letter home to my mother, telling her we were paying our way, and we were, thanks to the gifts people gave us. We still found bags of food on our doorstep two or three times a week. Fruit and vegetables, with sweets for the children, which Ros hid from them.

The families in the few houses around Lefkada frequently invited us to their homes for supper. Sometimes they did not eat until as late as ten o'clock, by which time the children, who had been constantly spoilt by our hosts from the moment we arrived, were no longer hungry and had fallen asleep. At midnight they wanted to wake up the children so we could all dance together to traditional Greek music. Maybe the islanders saw us as a family struggling to get by; the word was certainly out that I was looking for work.

I was already aware there was a simple economy on the island: to acquire no more than you needed with as little effort as possible. There was no sign of affluence, not in the housing, nor in the way anyone dressed, and very few people owned a car. It seemed that for many, to feed yourself and have a roof over your head was enough. And why not, if it freed you up to sit in the taverna and play *tavli* or fiddle with your *komboloi* (worry beads)? It was the women you saw working every day, taking pride in things, sweeping the steps or washing clothes. A man's life was to drink ouzo, talk politics and watch football on the communal televisions in the cafés.

᠊᠊᠊᠊᠊᠊᠊᠊ ⌐ ᠊᠊᠊᠊᠊᠊᠊᠊

In Maria's cramped little kitchen, amongst the pots and pans and the herbs hanging from the ceiling, was the only telephone for miles.

'Dad, how much longer?' asked Lysta, impatiently waiting to speak to Eleri.

'Any moment now.'

I had already told her she could have no more than five minutes, and suggested she write down all the things she wanted to say, which she had, the first being to tell Eleri that Ros was now her schoolteacher. But when the call came through she spoke so nervously I told her she would have to shout if Eleri was going to hear a single word she was saying.

She was embarrassed and told me to go away.

So I went and helped Maria to break up a block of frozen squid, which she then put into the sink and poured boiling water over. Once we'd finished, I told Lysta it was time to say goodbye.

As she put the phone down I asked, 'Do you feel better now?'

All she said was that Mrs Hughes, the PE teacher, had knocked herself out in the gym, Eleri's hamster had escaped, and the school bus had broken down taking them swimming in Caernarfon.

⌑

It was early spring and I'd noticed a softness in the breeze, a warmth that came and went depending on the direction of the wind. Honey bees, who did not share the Ikarian work ethic, were already busy in the yellow broom flowers.

I watched a single-sheared plough being pulled by a donkey, turning over the dry soil as the sun climbed over the small fields. I imagined this scene had probably not changed for a thousand years, the wife following her husband, throwing loose stones into a straw basket slung over the donkey's back.

There was no sign of life in the vineyards, just the bare vines all in neat straight lines stretching down the slopes, waiting for that surge of growth to unfurl their leaves. I thought there would probably be work for me here in the autumn, if we survived until then. I could see myself treading grapes, singing Greek songs with the old folk as the light faded over the Aegean.

⌑

Maria had asked me to tenderise a dozen octopus for a birthday party. It takes some energy to prepare them for cooking. They have to be thrown down repeatedly on a rocky surface, plunged into a bucket of sea water, then cleaned carefully without removing the suckers. It has to be done when they are fresh. By way of thanking me, she invited us for a free supper at the taverna.

What the children didn't know was that we were going to be eating goat, which was cheaper than lamb and the Ikarians loved. Ros thought they wouldn't eat it, because they had made friends with many of the wild goats, who were easy to approach, and had even given some of them names. I was sure Ros was right, so we pretended we were having lamb; it had never seemed to worry them to be eating what had been running around in the fields back in North Wales.

Luckily, just as Maria was serving us, Sam had something on his mind. He was deep in thought, searching for the right words.

'Dad,' he eventually said, 'how long does it take someone to grow up?'

One of those questions a developing boy likes to hurl at you out of the blue. He preferred it if I didn't answer straight away; that I had to think about it.

'Hmm, well, that's a tricky one. For some people it can take a lifetime, for others it can happen much faster. Why do you ask?'

'Because I feel I have grown up.'

'But you're only eight.'

'Yes, but I feel much older.'

'How much older?'

'Well, probably at least twelve.'

'So what is the point you are trying to make?'

'That I'm ready, Dad . . . I'm ready to go shopping on my own in Aghios Kirikos.'

'Wow. That's a big thing you're asking.'

'Please, Dad. It's only a half-hour walk, and I understand Greek money.'

I didn't know what to say, and waited for Ros to respond.

'I don't see why not,' she said. 'No harm is going to come to him.'

So Ros and I agreed it was a natural step for him to take. We had finished our meal, neither Sam nor Lysta having noticed we'd been eating a slightly different meat. I thought we had got away with it, until Maria came to clear the table. 'The goat, yes, you like?'

A look of horror came over their faces.

'Goat! We've eaten goat . . . no we haven't!' cried Lysta.

'Mum, it's not true, is it?'

If only Maria hadn't said anything. We had fallen into a pit and one not worth trying to dig ourselves out of. Lysta was particularly upset and Ros and I spent over fifteen minutes trying to console her. We promised them they would never have to eat goat again and ordered their favourite, spoons of vanilla paste in glasses of water, hoping that would cheer them up.

Sitting in the taverna, no matter who you were talking to, you were always drawn to the sea and the individual stars that appeared one by one in the darkening twilight. The expansive sunsets dispersed on the horizon while behind us the mountain peaks darkened. Eventually the dramatic afterglow faded as night came down upon us. Only then did your eye follow the distant lights of a ferry going back to Athens. No wonder it was so easy to drift away from the here and now. The sea seemed to lure you back into ancient myth, stirred the imagination; perhaps that's why Datsun Jim was always gazing into the distance. I realised I felt some sympathy for him. The past was so very much alive here that no one on the island was quite in the present day. I thought I'd found the answer to what was going on in Ikaria; it was all rather peculiar.

Involved in my own reverie, I hadn't noticed the man pulling a chair up next to me until he introduced himself.

'I am Spyros,' he said in a soft voice, shaking my hand with a relaxed, confident smile. I could tell by the smoothness of his palm that he did not work the land. He was handsome, with the distinguished look of a well-educated man, his hair whitening. 'Could I speak to you? I am fluent in English.'

'Yes, of course. But first, this is my wife Ros, and my children.'

'Lovely to meet you,' said Ros. 'I like your name.'

'Thank you. It was my father's name and my grandfather's,' he said. 'But please, forgive me, I am here to make you a proposition if you are interested.'

'I'll leave you two to talk,' Ros said, and took the children off to bed. Lysta was still upset, vowing that she would never eat meat again.

I didn't get a goodnight kiss from her, while I seemed to have been forgiven by Sam who gave me a hug.

Over a beer and a bowl of olives, Spyros told me about Sister Ulita, who lived alone in the monastery at Evaggelismos, just a kilometre away, above the road to Xylosirtis. On and off for the past two years he had been studying ancient religious scripts there, but was now returning to Athens. Although she was not old, the nun suffered from arthritic hands and was unable to milk her goats. She also needed someone to work the vegetable garden and look after the orchard. There were many old fruit trees that needed tending.

'Why is she all alone at the monastery?' I asked. 'What happened to the monks?'

'It is a long story, so I will shorten it for you. The monks over the years gradually died, and to keep the monastery open nuns were sent from Mykonos and they too died one by one until only Sister Ulita and the Mother Superior were left. The Mother Superior returned to Mykonos, and that is why Sister Ulita is alone. It is difficult for her to find anyone reliable, and as you know, goats have to be milked twice a day.'

'But I am not a religious man,' I told him.

'That is not important.'

'Will she pay me?'

'There is no money, but she will pay you with food and fruit. She makes goat's cheese and yoghurt. You can feed your whole family on what the monastery provides. Remember, it is cheap to live here.'

'I'd like to meet her. I'm used to that kind of work.'

'Good, then let's go tomorrow. Is eight in the morning OK for you?'

'Will that be eight or eight thirty?' I asked him.

'Ha! You're getting to know the Ikarians already. It will be at eight, I promise you.'

As Maria brought Spyros another beer, she told me Stelios was on the telephone, wanting to speak to me.

'Tomorrow,' he said, 'we go night fishing under the stars. The weather is good, but you bring warm clothes, you understand.'

'What time?'

'At six. Don't be late.'

It was eleven by the time I got into bed, waking Ros despite tiptoeing as quietly as I could. She told me Lysta had left a note beside the bed written in block capitals. I WILL NOT EAT MEAT AGAIN.

'So our daughter's become a vegetarian. What did Sam say about it?'

'He said if Dad stops eating meat then so will he.'

As we were dropping off to sleep, Ros whispered to me, 'Are you glad we came?'

I didn't need to think about it. 'Yes, I am. Are you?'

'I love it. I feel at home on Ikaria.'

'So you want to stay?'

'For as long as we can. Maybe we could buy a house here.'

The next morning Spyros was waiting for me, sitting at the same table drinking coffee and smoking a Camel cigarette.

'You did not smoke last night,' I said to him as Maria brought me a black Nescafé, placing her hand gently on my head. She liked to pat me at least once a day. It was her little way of showing her affection for me.

'No, I have my own smoking habit. I smoke only three cigarettes a day, one in the morning, then again with my lunch, and the last at six o'clock. I have done this for over twenty years.'

'But why have one so early in the morning?' I asked.

'Because a habit will always come looking for you, and after I have conceded to it, I can get on with my day.' He laughed. 'Then it can wait for me.'

'That is unusual.'

'I enjoy each one, and I'm always looking forward to the next,' he said, turning his gaze to the sea. Clearly a thoughtful man, he went on, 'Did you know the Aegean has the same four temperaments as man? Look at her: today she is phlegmatic . . . but tomorrow, who knows?'

We finished our coffee and made our way to the monastery, a twenty-five-minute walk in the warming sunshine. I had left my jacket at home; I'd felt it first thing, the bite no longer in the wind. Spyros had his shirt half undone, showing a mass of grey hairs, and soon sweat started to appear on his brow as the sun climbed. I noticed a lizard running across the path in front of us, the first one I had seen since we'd arrived. Its tail left a pattern in the dust as it scurried past. The air was full of the smell of dried herbs, little bushes of them that rattled in the wind. Small yellow and purple flowers had appeared, spring pushing up from the undergrowth, delicate buds forming on the fig trees.

The solid, dark green gates of the monastery were closed, tall and forbidding, cast into the high stone wall, giving an overriding sense of exclusion. No doubt the monks had needed protection from the world outside and the pirates who used to invade Ikaria, but I could only imagine what a desperate and weary traveller must have felt coming to seek refuge here. Spyros pulled on the chain and the jangle of a bell could be heard some way off, fading away into silence. We looked at each other and waited.

At least two minutes passed before the gate slowly opened and a nun appeared. Spyros introduced me in Greek as she put her small hand in mine.

'Sister Ulita, *kali mera*,' I said with my best Greek pronunciation.

There was little to see of her, enveloped as she was in her black habit; only the olive skin of her cheeks and her perfect teeth, revealed by a bright smile. She was wearing sunglasses. It was hard to get any idea of her age, with so much of her hidden; even her forehead was covered. She beckoned us into a courtyard and sat us at a slate table in the shade of some cypress trees.

I noticed her swollen hands as she poured the coffee and pushed a bowl of sugar cubes towards me. A smile seemed to be her permanent expression. Spyros asked me to forgive him but he had to speak in Greek to explain things to her. 'I want to tell her all about you. It is important.'

She sat listening, stroking a well-fed cat, unlike all the others I'd seen, purring on her lap. There was a ring on her finger that surely she could not remove over the swollen joint. They talked at length without my understanding a word, but from time to time she acknowledged me with a smile and a brief touch of her hand on mine. She seemed intriguing and mysterious, because there was so little of her on show. She spoke to me in Greek, not knowing a word of English, Spyros telling me she wanted to know if I was happy to work for food.

'*Ochi khrimata*,' she said, waving her finger.

'No money,' I said back to her. Words I'd heard from Datsun Jim.

'Tell her,' I said to Spyros, 'we have to learn each other's language.'

We walked around the grounds of the monastery, along a path edged with rose bushes, buds unfolding into pink petals. There was a stepped vegetable garden, through which a zigzagging water course traversed each row of plants. There were trays of seedlings in raised square beds under glass panes. We walked on into an old orchard of peach trees, plums and pears, amongst them a few brightly coloured beehives.

'You can eat whatever you want: figs, bananas, pomegranates as well.'

I met the goats she wanted me to milk, a breed I did not recognise, mottled and grey, tethered by a rope and eating hay. Spyros told me that they needed to be moved as well as milked twice daily.

'They eat a circle of grass; we do not have fields as you do in England.'

At this point the nun put her hands together.

'Mr Neeko,' she said.

'What is wrong?' I asked.

'She is praying you will come and save her life,' said Spyros.

'Save her life! What does she mean?'

'That you will come and work at the monastery.'

'Tell her I don't know yet. I must talk to my wife.'

It would have been easy to say yes without a second thought. But there was another side to me now, one who lived on the land, and the other who wanted to go to sea and be a fisherman. I would have to split my life between the two. There was an answer, and it lay with Ros, for she could milk two goats just as well as me. And so I replied as an Ikarian would.

'*Avrio*. I will let you know tomorrow.'

'Yes, of course, and you are to bring your wife and children for lunch,' Spyros translated.

On the walk back to Lefkada I asked him whether the nun had ever taken off her sunglasses in all the time he had worked with her.

'No,' he said. 'Never once, not even on a cloudy winter's day. She always wears them.'

When I got home, Ros was hanging washing on the line, an old rope strung between two pine trees in front of the house. She told me Sam had left at nine o'clock that morning to walk to Aghios Kirikos carrying a shopping bag. That was three hours ago.

'Don't you think you should go and look for him?'

Neither of us felt there was anything really to worry about, but I went in search of him anyway. We both thought I'd find him in a taverna with a family who had taken him under their wing, feasting on a large lunch. I'd only been on the road ten minutes when Datsun Jim pulled up beside me, his pick-up stacked high with crates of chickens. I managed to squeeze in next to an elderly lady, dressed in black robes, with a cockerel on her lap. She said nothing, calmly stroking its feathers, not even turning her head to give me a look as I tried to manoeuvre myself into a comfortable position beside her. A cheap plastic crucifix swung from the rear-view mirror. Along the dashboard was an assortment of religious figures and glued to the car radio a small golden statue of the Virgin Mary. Beneath me, several girlie magazines slipped out from under the seat. On the front cover of one a girl with large breasts was holding what looked like a medieval ball and chain. I wondered whether the solemn woman beside me, her harsh features clearly not given to smiling, was Datsun Jim's grandmother. What an enigmatic lot these Ikarians were. Words were not bandied about; on the whole journey Datsun Jim only uttered a single syllable, pointing at the bird.

'Cock.'

'Yes, cock,' I said, trying to push back with my heel the incriminating material that slid out from under the seat every time he put his foot on the brake.

We arrived at Aghios Kirikos without another word being spoken. Not a look from the old lady as I thanked them for the lift into town; maybe she was deaf rather than antisocial.

Now I had to find Sam, and headed to the main square where most of the cafés and tavernas were. I walked past tables full of unshaven men playing *tavli* with raised voices and dramatic gestures, drinking ouzo or coffee. They must have been talking politics; football doesn't drive you that crazy, or maybe it did out here. Bare-footed children were throwing stones at cats, and to complete the cacophony teenage boys circled the square on whining mopeds showing off to their girlfriends.

At the kiosk I looked at the newspaper headlines; the only information I could glean was the trouble still existing between Greece and Turkey. I'd lost touch with the world since we'd been here, and without a radio, newspapers or television had no idea what was going on back home. I missed none of it. There was one weekly newspaper in English, the *Athens News*, which condensed international politics into a few pages. I only ever flicked through it in the kiosk, looking for the football results, hoping Spurs had won, and I always tried to put it back as neatly as possible. If I was spotted I would go to the counter and buy a packet of chewing gum. It was the cheapest thing on sale and buying it eased my guilt.

I couldn't find Sam anywhere. I could see Ikaria's entire police force, according to Stelios – the two policemen playing *tavli* – but I saw no point in disturbing them. Just as I was about to make my way back to Ros, I heard Stamati shouting my name, running from his kitchen in vest and apron.

'I wait for you at the weekend, and you do not come.'

I apologised. Had he really been expecting me?

'Your boy, he came this morning and I asked him, where is your father? And he says you have gone to the monastery.'

'It's true, I did go to the monastery, but can you tell me where Sam is now?'

'You go there searching for God?'

'No, for work. Do you know where my boy is?'

Stamati hadn't seen him since the morning, walking with Christos, the son of a local schoolteacher.

'They are a good family. Do not worry, they will bring him to your house.'

I decided to go home, and it wasn't long before I was re-united with Sam. A couple of kilometres from Aghios Kirikos I heard behind me the repetitive sound of a beeping horn and loud cheering. I turned round and saw an old red Fiat coming towards me, hands waving extravagantly from the car windows. As they pulled up I could see Sam sitting amongst three other children on the back seat, clutching his bag of shopping. The husband and wife greeted me like a long-lost friend.

'He's a beautiful boy,' the woman said, as I lifted Sam from the back seat. I ignored her and was waiting instead for an apology for stealing a child for nearly seven hours. But none was offered and before I'd said a word they had driven off, leaving us in a cloud of dust. You could have said it was a case of kidnapping, but here it was part of everyday life. The islanders loved children, and seemed to think they belonged to everyone. It was something we were going to have to get used to. In England half the police force would have been out looking for him.

As we walked back to Lefkada, Sam said he realised how worried Mum would be.

'I just couldn't get away, Dad, and then we went and played football on the beach.'

'That must have been fun.'

'It was. He kept calling me Bobby Charlton.'

'Has it put you off going shopping on your own?'

'Well, maybe I'm not that grown up after all.'

'You mean you're not twelve?'

'More like ten.'

5

Night Fishing

Ros was nervous again. No matter how much I reassured her, she had a feeling of foreboding about my going night fishing with Stelios. It was my spatial awareness that concerned her; apparently, I didn't have any. She had dreamt last night that I had fallen overboard, but I brushed it aside, telling her dreams didn't come true and I knew how to look after myself. She pleaded with me to wear a life jacket and I promised I would; I didn't mention that I hadn't worn one on the last trip.

We had talked about us sharing the work at the monastery, and she was happy to milk the goats if I was working with Datsun Jim or Stelios. It would fit well into her daily routine, before she took up her schoolteaching duties. The more work the better, and Ros knew how to milk goats as she had often milked Frieda, our house cow, back at Dyffryn; she was looking forward to it.

'Life here has a beautiful simplicity,' she said. 'So uncomplicated, the children not glued to a television screen, happily amusing themselves in the natural world. I'm so glad we came,' she said, hugging me, 'especially after Pa's death.'

I hadn't told Ros we had spent all but fifty pounds of our capital and unless there was a dramatic change in my rate of pay I would have to get in touch with Jack. Luckily in amongst all the news from home in my mother's last letter, she had given me his telephone number.

We spent hardly anything on food, but when we needed to buy medicines they were expensive, having to be imported from Athens. The pharmacist in Aghios kept talking Ros into trying his recommended remedies for those minor ailments that children get, like sore throats and runny noses; everything, of course, was written in Greek, so we never knew what we were taking. But we trusted him. He looked the part, with a white coat and a pair of smart horn-rimmed glasses, and, after all, it is by their appearance that you judge people.

And the children were growing out of their clothes and shoes. At least with the weather warming up every day they could run around in flip-flops. Life is cheaper when the weather is hot. But razor blades were dear, so I only shaved twice a week. With a few days' growth on my chin I already had the dishevelled look of an Ikarian.

When I met Stelios he was sitting on the side of the boat with his head in his hands, deep in thought. Beside him in a plastic bucket were bottles of retsina and some bread and fruit. He half acknowledged me, raising an arm, but that was it. I tried to get his attention by asking if Theo was coming with us, but all I got was a dismissive wave of the hand. Eventually I said, 'You're not in a good mood this evening.'

'Yeah, yeah, I'm all right,' he said.

'Are we going fishing?'

'It is the weather, maybe not so good.'

'Is there a storm coming?' I asked.

'I think if we go early and put the nets down we can shelter until it blows out.'

'Do we have to take the risk?'

'I need the money. There are repairs I have to do.'

He lit a cigarette. 'In case it gets rough I will tie a rope around you.' I wondered whether he was being serious. He then inflated a rubber dinghy with a foot pump, telling me we would row to shore once the nets were down.

'Do we have life jackets?' I asked, thinking of Ros and her sense of foreboding. I tried to shrug off any apprehension, telling myself that Stelios knew what he was doing.

'Of course we have life jackets,' he said, 'in the cabin. Take one later and put it over your oilskin.'

In the fading light, we moved through the water, the twilight spilling its blood-red colours into the ink of the night. The sky filled with stars, luminous and sparkling over the Aegean. We soon lost sight of Ikaria, the sea not even rippled, but like a dark plain that we surged through, the only white water breaking over the bow. Stelios started to sing a reflective song that seemed to suit his mood.

He increased the revs and the boat thudded against the water. We were now without landmarks and the night embraced us. I was filled with a nervous excitement for what lay ahead. I'd put on an oilskin jacket over a thick pullover; my eyes wept in the biting air. Not a wave ruffled the surface, and I could stand easily without having to cling onto anything. Ahead in the darkness I could see distant pinpricks of light. I realised we must have been at sea for at least an hour as gradually they became houses, lit high up on the cliffs of Samos. Here we let down the nets and watched them sink beneath us.

Stelios pulled the dinghy close beside the boat and told me to get in, passing me the bucket of food and retsina, a bag of fish and a bundle of twigs. A breath of wind swept across my face as we rowed quietly to a small sandy cove, where the eddying currents caused waves to swell and carried us effortlessly to the shore. For some reason I felt we were breaking the law, that we were up to something illegal and at any moment we were going to be discovered. I suppose it went with the night, the silence and being under cover of darkness.

In the moonlight, we found a sheltered spot beneath the cliffs. Although we had enough twigs to start a fire, Stelios sent me off to look for wood. It seemed an impossible task in a stony landscape without a tree to be seen, until he pointed out a half-demolished hut up on the headland that must once have housed some livestock, where I found a couple of half-rotten planks.

He lit our fire in a circle of stones, then laid barbunia across a wooden grill. As they cooked, he turned them with two sticks he'd sharpened with his penknife.

We drank retsina and I felt an elemental connection to the things around me: the air, the water, the fire, the smell of grilling fish. I watched the gentle rocking of the boat some fifty yards from the shore, a single beam of light shining from the mast. We ate the barbunia between our fingers, Stelios staring intently into the flames, as if his own thoughts danced before his eyes. He talked about Theo and how since he had fallen in love he couldn't think straight. He wasted his time talking to girls sitting on the harbour wall, and didn't have the courage to tell the one who had stolen his heart how he felt, so he showed off to them all.

'It is no good. He shouts at his mother and has no interest in work.'

'It's something we all have to go through,' I said, a rather lame response, but I didn't know what else to say.

'On Ikaria the girls want husbands and marry boys before they have become men.'

He paused and lit a cigarette, 'Of course, he thinks it is love,' turning to me with a knowing smile. 'Yes . . . and then after they have children the woman gets fat and the man becomes miserable, so he plays *tavli* and drinks ouzo.'

'Theo is no different from any other man, Stelios. Let him live. You're sounding too much like an older brother,' I said.

'Well, maybe you are right. I only tell you because it happened to me.'

Then, as if to cheer himself up, he laughed, a self-deprecating laugh, and stamped out the fire, singing '*Pende pano, pende cato*'.

What I should never have done, as he rowed us back to the boat, was put my hand on his shoulder and say, 'It looks as though we've been lucky,' meaning there would be no storm that night. Stelios knew better than to acknowledge such a remark. And within five minutes I regretted it. In the far distance a flash of jagged lightning split the darkness like cracks of light fracturing glass. We hurriedly brought up the last of the nets and put the catch in the hold as the storm blew closer. The sea began to rise up like great watery hillsides, and Stelios grabbed a rope and tied one end around my waist and the other to the mast.

I hadn't got a life jacket on and couldn't get one now. Stelios was holding the tiller, trying to steer the boat into the waves, but they broke over us, such a volume of water that I thought the boat would break in two. We lost the dinghy, which tumbled away across the sea, blown out of reach like a child's toy. I was being thrown across the deck and couldn't make my voice heard when I shouted to Stelios, wanting to know what the hell I was meant to be doing. As I tried to make my way towards him, a great wall of solid water swept me over the side and hurled me into the sea. I had gone overboard.

What went through my mind at that moment was not fear or panic but the need to keep myself afloat, which I did by managing to do the breast stroke and keep my head above water. I was still secured by the rope and could see the light swaying chaotically on the mast. At times I seemed to be just an arm's length from the boat, then suddenly I would be sucked backwards, carried upwards and find myself looking down on it. Stelios grabbed the rope and began pulling me in, his legs braced on either side of the mast, hauling me ever closer. I grasped one of the tyres, but I hadn't the strength to climb back on board. At last Stelios managed to get hold of my oilskin and somehow heave me over the side, rolling me like a sack of potatoes on to the deck, and then dragging me to the hold. He untied the rope and closed the hatch over me as I crouched, shivering, gasping for breath, my arms around the engine, hugging it for warmth. And that's where I spent the next two hours, my eyes on a level with the words embossed on the little plaque, *Made by Listers of Derby*. I hugged that throbbing motor all the way back to Aghios Kirikos, put my back against it, lay on top of it, wrapped myself around it. God, I thought, I've become emotionally attached to an engine. That dark space I now inhabited was my little bit of England. Sloshing around me were the spilt contents of the catch, a graveyard of fish, the octopus tangling up in each other, performing a macabre dance on the other side of life, the squid slithering from side to side, the barbunia the colour of sunsets, their scales glittering in a splinter of light. What was going on above me in that other world, I had no idea.

Stelios had enough to do without looking in on me. I felt as though I was living in an aquarium. What my body had gone through I didn't really know, but oddly I had moved from numbness to feeling extremely cold. I vibrated with it and couldn't close my mouth. I had also lost my grip and had no sensation in my feet, as if they had walked away from me in search of a better life. I had become the individual parts of myself, no longer a physical whole.

When everything stopped sliding all over the place I knew we'd survived the night. But I never let go of that motor, not until it slowed and shuddered to a stop and I could hear voices which must have been coming from the quayside.

Then Stelios lifted the hatch. Piercing light shone into the darkness and the salt in my eyes suddenly burnt furiously. It was too painful to bear and I shouted to Stelios '*Nero, nero*' and he came and poured fresh water all over my eyes and face, a whole bottle of it.

If Ros had been there I'm sure we would have been heading home on the next ferry. That clairvoyant wife of mine who had seen it all happening. I asked Stelios if he could get me some dry clothes.

'I cannot go home like this.'

'Hey, we have made it, be happy, you have your life! Come, here you are,' he said, passing me a bundle someone had brought from his pick-up.

All around us on the quayside were fishermen who had not ventured out into that angry sea. It could well have been a biblical scene, the wise welcoming back the foolish. It was one of those moments when I wished I could understand every word being said. Did they think Stelios was a fool? I would never know. But then those same fishermen started to unload the catch and maybe that was what they always did: helped each other out.

In some of Stelios's clothes that were too small for me I said goodbye to him. I could tell from his look that he was waiting to hear me say 'never again' and that I'd be on my way with a final 'thanks for the experience'.

But I didn't. Instead I said, 'Will we go out again this week?' and he threw his arms around me and said, 'You know, I see it in you now, a man whose strength lives inside him.'

As he handed me a bag of fish, he asked, 'Will you tell your wife?'

I had to think about that. 'Not all of it, not in the way it happened.'

'She would not let you come again?'

'Were you frightened, Stelios? Tell me the truth.'

'Oh, my friend, I did not have time to be frightened,' and he laughed, that laugh that rolled like the sea.

Ros was waking when I walked in and fell into bed beside her.

'I'm back,' I said, 'back from the sea, and yes I did fall overboard.'

Better to say it quickly and flippantly and get it over and done with. I just told her I was in the water for a few seconds with a rope around me.

'Thank goodness you were wearing a life jacket! I was so worried when I heard the wind get up in the night.'

It would have been an outright lie to say anything about the jacket, but when you know how someone is going to react, and that the whole truth will cause them anxiety, life has taught me it's best to give a watered-down version and sprinkle it with a little humour. Ros was quite happy with my fisherman's tale, even laughing occasionally at my light-hearted story. I leant over and gave her a kiss. She had no idea how relieved I felt to be home.

'You smell of diesel and seaweed,' she said, sniffing my neck. 'And whose clothes are you wearing?'

Then Sam burst into the room. 'Dad did you bring home some barbunia? I love barbunia,' he said, and then Lysta appeared at the door.

'Well I don't. I'm a vegetarian.'

I told Lysta we'd heard enough of that now, so instead she told me how the previous evening Seth hadn't been able to go to sleep, because a bat kept flying around the room. That probably explained why he hadn't surfaced yet.

Ros told them it was time for school and they left me to sleep. Because of the warmer weather the classroom was now outside, so I closed the shutters and slipped away into some deep-sea dreaming.

I could have gone on sleeping; Ros tried to wake me but it took all my children jumping on the bed before I realised we should be going to the monastery that morning.

I quickly got dressed and we all went down to the taverna

where Spyros was waiting for us. We told him our plan about working for Sister Ulita: that Ros and I would share the work. He was delighted. 'If you knew how many have let her down.' And so we all walked up to meet the nun, who greeted us with a warmth that overflowed into joy as we introduced her to the children, who each in turn received her blessing. Was it just us, or did every visitor to the monastery get such a welcome?

Ros loved the whole atmosphere of the place, calling it the 'Garden of Eden', and when Sister Ulita took us to see the goats Lysta was won over immediately. We walked through the gardens, Sister Ulita naming in Greek every tree we passed. The little church she showed us could seat no more than two dozen people; there was a gold-encrusted cross on the altar and painted icons of the saints staring down from the whitewashed walls, while the bright sunlight illuminated the stained-glass windows. We could imagine what a relief it would be to escape into this cool sanctuary in the hot days of summer.

We drank tea in the shade of the cypress trees in the courtyard and tasted her homemade sweet bergamot, which the children loved.

'How do you say in Greek, may we have some more, please?' asked Lysta.

'*Boroume na echoume ligo perissotero, parakalo?*' said Spyros, which Lysta tried to repeat, until she got completely tongue-tied.

Then we got down to earthly matters and Spyros explained our plan. Sister Ulita listened intently, nodding her head with a broadening smile, and finally clasped her hands and sighed, recognising that we had reached an agreement. While Spyros translated the happiness she felt, she went back to the kitchen and returned with jars of fresh yoghurt and honey and some more sweet bergamot for Lysta. She told us it was all from the monastery and for us to take home.

🏮

A couple of days later, as we were lying in bed, both of us waking from a good night's sleep, Ros suddenly asked, 'So what is our financial situation at the moment?'

We'd never arranged it, but throughout our marriage most of our serious conversations had taken place in bed, either just before sleep or first thing in the morning.

I was taken completely by surprise this time and didn't have an immediate answer, because she'd never asked such a direct question about our cash flow before. Whenever we'd needed something, she would ask whether we could buy a sofa, a carpet, or whatever it was, and I would reply that I'd check the bank balance. That was when we were farming, of course, but all the cash we had now was in a money belt so I could hardly say I didn't know.

Ros's question brought into the open a situation I had hoped would be resolved without involving her. My problem was Datsun Jim and the two and a half thousand drachma he owed me. I'd asked him when he was going to pay up several times. It was always *avrio* and I'd had enough of it, so I'd told him I was resigning from my position of cement mixer. He didn't know the word resign, so I said, 'Finito, I'm finished,' which again he didn't understand. I looked through my phrase book but couldn't find an appropriate translation and ended up using the German, *kaputt*, which to my surprise he recognised.

'Please, you wait a little longer,' was his response, and I told him that was exactly what I had been doing. He told me again the money was on its way from his brother in Detroit. What choice did I have? If I walked away I doubted there was any chance of ever seeing it. So I didn't resign and said I would work for one more week, for which he gave me another of his awful hugs, which I always tried to avoid, because the smell of him lingered.

That was the situation I was in; all of my own making, I knew. What was I going to say to Ros, looking at me so optimistically?

'Why do you ask?'

'Well, if we can afford it, I was thinking we could go to Samos for a weekend. It's not that far away and it would be nice to visit another island.'

'That's a lovely idea . . . an extremely lovely idea . . .'

'But?'

This was the difficult bit, when I had to sound convincing but not over elaborate, otherwise I'd dig myself deeper into trouble.

'I'm just waiting for Datsun Jim to settle his account.'

'Settle his account?' said Ros. 'He doesn't have an account. He pays you in cash.'

'That's true, but he's waiting for some money to arrive, and as soon as it comes I can see no reason why we shouldn't have an exciting weekend in Samos. I hear the wine is very good.'

Ros gave me a look that said it all. 'We haven't got any money, have we? How much does he actually owe you?'

At that moment I decided to tell her everything. The only reason I ever held back from telling Ros the brutal truth about our finances was because of the anxiety I knew it would cause her. When we were farming and I thought we were heading for bankruptcy I kept it to myself. But what was the point now? It was hardly a dire situation that was going to ruin us. It was annoying, but if things ever got desperate Jack would help us out.

'Two and a half thousand drachma,' I told her.

'That would keep us going for ten days.'

'I know, but I've given him one more week.'

But the week was already three days old, and Ros was doubtful we would see a penny of it.

After one of those sleepless nights when something you should have dealt with gets magnified out of all proportion, I decided I could put it off no longer. I would have to ring Jack and get him to wire some money over. Those night fears had got hold of me: what if one of us suddenly needed urgent hospital treatment? What did our insurance cover? Would we have to pay up front and put in a claim later? This was all triggered, of course, by Datsun Jim. So I was up early.

It was our ninth anniversary, Lysta had told me yesterday. Nine years, not of total bliss, but on a scale of one to ten I'd give it nine, which is good.

I didn't know how Ros would score it; probably far less, as I had always had an eye on the next venture, although she had never actually told me she'd rather I worked a nine-to-five job.

I was sure there wasn't a florist on Ikaria so I wanted to cut her some flowers myself and crept out of the house while she slept. I didn't know the time, but it must have been before seven o'clock because Maria wasn't about and her kitchen door was still closed. I could easily open it because it was never locked, although she pulled a bolt across it on windy nights, only in case a storm blew up, not to keep anyone out, except maybe the goats. There was hardly any crime on the island and I'd never seen the two policemen out investigating anything. I found a pair of scissors and went in search of some of the wild flowers that grew around Lefkada. There were lots, including lupins, which I knew Ros liked. Apparently, when the Ikarians were starving during the Second World War, they ate lupin seeds, which must have been a risky business because they could be extremely poisonous if they weren't cooked properly.

When I got back to the taverna with my bouquet of flowers, Maria was up. I gave her back the scissors and told her Ros and I had been married nine years, a long time. Then I said it in Greek, '*ennea chronia*', which brought a smile to her face.

I said it again, '*Ennea chronia, Maria,*' and that made her laugh.

'Me and Yannis,' she said, '*saranta dyo chronia,*' which I later found out was forty-two years. I went and acknowledged it to her that evening, because I knew no one else who had been married that long.

When I gave Ros the flowers and said happy anniversary, she was genuinely touched that I had remembered and we went for an early morning swim. Ros reminded me of the first time we spent a night together, when I had to help her pull off her knee-length boots.

'How could I forget? It was in that flat you rented in Redcliffe Gardens.'

'And now here we are, swimming in the Aegean.'

The children were up when we returned, Lysta and Maria boiling eggs together. The taverna was empty. We usually had breakfast at home, but today was a special day. Maria brought us some slices of cake and sat with us, and we all had to hold hands while she muttered something in Greek.

'What did you say, Maria?'

'My mother, she taught me this, to bring you continued happiness.'

That evening I went back to the taverna to book a telephone call to Jack. On my own, I sat and drank retsina, a taste I had now become accustomed to. Maria would put a bottle on the table without my having to order it, together with some olives and a little dish of meze: a cube of feta and a mouthful of salt fish, both on small chunks of bread. I had become completely used to this generous and civilised Greek custom of providing tasty morsels with drinks. It suited me well; I much preferred not to drink on an empty stomach.

I searched in my pocket for some loose change to pay her, but she brushed me aside and gave me a hundred and fifty drachma for the octopus and squid that I'd brought back from my last fishing trip with Stelios. She hadn't told me that she'd added them to her menu because she needed the space in the fridge. It was totally unexpected and couldn't have come at a better time; it quite lifted my spirits. I could have hugged her.

🖼

It was impossible to get into bed quietly, because the springs beneath our thin mattress possessed a life of their own; they moved up and down the musical scale like an orchestra tuning up. Fidgeting about before finally getting comfortable only disturbed the other person, as the disjointed overture twanged beneath us. Also I was too long for the bed, my feet sticking out six inches. We had put up with the mattress and the dripping tap for three months, and for some reason tonight Ros said she'd had enough.

'We could do better for ourselves,' she said, looking around our very basic bare room. No electricity, not a picture on the walls. We were living in a box. 'We need to find somewhere else. Somewhere that feels like a home.'

That was going to cost money, but Ros was right: it was time to move on. I told her that I'd booked a call to Jack, to ask him to transfer some money.

'Has Datsun Jim paid up yet?' she asked.

'No, he hasn't. I'll sort it out with him tomorrow.' That's if we bumped into each other.

As we dropped off to sleep, with the odd twang still sounding beneath us, I whispered in Ros's ear, 'Was it Bach who wrote "Air on a bed spring"?'

6

The Potato Boat

June on Ikaria, and it felt as if we were making a new beginning. We were moving, no more than a hundred yards down the road; to be precise, from one side of the taverna to the other. Into a single-storey house that stood above an unkempt garden, with rusting, cast-iron steps that led onto a veranda covered in dry eucalyptus leaves. Hanging precariously above this was rotting wooden lattice-work that had once supported a vine. It swayed in the breeze like an old hammock. There's something melancholic about things that have seen better days. The flaky, blue shutters needed to be opened so new life could be breathed into the dusty interior: four large rooms with peeling walls that had faded to a sullen yellow.

There was no electricity, but who needed it; the days were long and hot. It had a lavatory of sorts, at the back of the house, which you flushed with a bucket of water, and it was owned by a cousin of Maria's, who said we could have it rent free if we painted it. We didn't hesitate, after living in what now seemed like a cell for several months. Maria said the house had been empty for over two years, which explained why it was an insects' graveyard. Other forms of wildlife had perished in here too; the skeletal remains of a goat lay on the floor of one room, and when Lysta saw it she let it be known she would definitely not be sleeping in there.

Obese spiders quivered in their webs, with trapped prey they couldn't be bothered to feast upon. Bodies crunched beneath us as we made our way from room to room, and while for the rest of us this was not the most pleasant experience, Seth was fascinated by these flattened corpses. Picking them up, he inspected their delicate remains between his fingers.

I'd noticed this in him before in Wales. He seemed to have a natural interest in little dead things. He definitely didn't get that from my genes.

'Well,' said Ros, hands on hips, looking around the room, weighing up exactly what we were taking on, 'we're going to need gallons of paint, turps, rollers, ladders. Who's going to paint the ceilings?' Obviously me, by the look on her face.

'I can do that by fixing a roller to a broom handle,' I said, having behind me the experience of painting every ceiling in our farmhouse.

'We can paint, Mum,' said Sam and Lysta.

'Well, they could do the skirting boards,' I suggested, 'and some of the walls, as far as they can reach.'

'I could stand on a chair, Dad,' Sam said, at his helpful best.

I pointed out that we didn't have a chair, or any furniture . . . we had nothing apart from our clothes and a couple of sleeping bags.

'Well, let's get on with it,' said Ros. 'Lysta, in your neatest handwriting let's make a list of everything we're going to need.'

We estimated it would take three weeks to make the place habitable. There was no hurry, we could move in bit by bit. Or as the Ikarians would say, *siga siga* (slowly slowly).

At least we had some money again. I'd had my phone call with Jack. Such was the delay on the line, it was as if we were speaking to one another from different planets. I kept hearing my own words coming back to me, just as Jack was beginning his reply. It was hopeless and both of us lost patience. In the end I bawled down the phone, 'Be quiet for a moment. Just don't say anything.' And he didn't, like a good brother, and I told him we needed some money. So he wired it over and a week later I picked it up from the only bank in Aghios Kirikos.

The first thing we bought was a mattress that I ordered

from Tassos, an unusual young man in that he obviously took great care of his appearance. Clean and tidy with a neat haircut and smelling of aftershave, he was unlike any other Ikarian we had seen.

His furniture shop was also unusual, because there was no furniture in it. In fact, he had nothing in his shop, only the chair he sat on, and a little book for writing orders in duplicate. He liked using the word duplicate, randomly dropping it into any conversation. When I asked him why he had no items on show, he said he couldn't afford them. I ordered our mattress from a catalogue, and Tassos said it would take a couple of weeks for it to come from Athens. He charged us one thousand eight hundred drachma, which was about thirty pounds.

Ros was pleased, but thought we ought to have tried it first. I told her not to worry, that any mattress after the spongy old thing we'd been sleeping on for months would be an improvement.

Three weeks later, when it still hadn't arrived, I went back to the shop and saw it leaning up against the back wall and asked Tassos when he was going to deliver it. He just raised his shoulders the way Italians do when they say '*No comprendi*', and looked at me vacantly.

'We never talked about delivery,' he said. 'My price was for the mattress.'

It was another one of those frustrating Ikarian moments when I had to weigh up whether it was worth the effort of trying to resolve a misunderstanding. I could tell immediately that Tassos didn't care about customer relations, so there the mattress stayed.

Early the next morning I was sitting with a coffee at the taverna when Datsun Jim turned up. He hadn't paid me a single drachma, and I had told him again, nearly two weeks ago, that I wouldn't work for him any more, but he still wasn't taking no for an answer. You'd have thought by his reaction I was the guilty party. He broke down, giving a performance an actor in a Greek tragedy would have been proud of.

'One more week, please, one more week, then my brother will be here to pay you.'

I didn't think I could bear to hear him say that again.

In the back of the pick-up he had a bath and a lavatory. They were brand new, still wrapped in cellophane.

'How can I lift these into the house without you to help me?' he pleaded.

He pulled out the lining of his trouser pockets.

'Look, no money, my dear friend. Yesterday I sell a goat to put petrol in the pick-up.'

I couldn't walk away from him; I told him I would come and help, but only to unload the bath and lavatory and put them in place.

'That's it. No more! And then you will come to Aghios Kirikos and pick up my mattress for me.'

When I told Ros what I was going to do and that I'd be back in a couple of hours, I could see in her eyes that she doubted it.

As we were driving to the house, I asked Datsun Jim why his brother hadn't sent him the money he had always promised.

'He has much money in America, but the banks he says are thieves. He does not like this, so he is bringing it himself in a suitcase, to pay everyone.'

Maybe it was the truth. When Jack wired over five hundred pounds, they had taken thirty-five in bank charges.

'And this brother . . . what is his name again?'

'Giorgos.'

'Will he be angry with you for not finishing the house?'

'Yes, he will go crazy, and there will be a big fight.'

In the June sunshine, either end of a spanking new bath, we

shuffled along a dusty path through the olive trees. I looked up at the house Jim was building: no roof, each room visible in the open façade. Why install a bath now? It made no sense whatsoever. An image came to mind of Jim's brother sitting in the bath wearing a plastic cap, on full show to everyone, scrubbing his back, shouting out 'Kali mera' to anyone who passed. Worse still would be him sitting on the lavatory. That's how it was on Ikaria; nothing seemed to be thought through. I wished Ros could understand that Jim was completely out of his depth.

The bathroom was on the first floor. Halfway up the stairs, struggling with the bath that we had somehow managed to inch through the empty doorways, we heard somebody shouting up from the garden. 'Kali mera, Jim. Ti kanis?' What are you up to?

Fairly obvious, I would have thought. But Jim had to stop and chat, while I held on to the bath, and another ten minutes had been taken out of the morning before at last we reached our goal.

'Are you sure this is the bathroom?' I asked.

It looked unlikely.

'Where is the plumbing?'

'Yes, plumbing? What is this word? I do not understand it.'

'Where are the pipes, Jim?'

'I am not fitting the pipes.'

I asked him again. 'Are you sure this is the bathroom?'

'Yes, yes, I am sure. The room with a little round window.'

After we had put the lavatory in place, probably an hour later, Jim gave me one of his awful embraces. Fortunately he didn't smell so bad that day.

'You are like a brother to me,' he said.

'I don't feel like one,' I replied. Fool came to mind.

'We go for a drink now.'

'No, not for a drink. Now you are going to do something for me.'

So Datsun Jim and I drove to Tassos's shop and picked up the mattress. We had to lean it up against the cement mixer, and it bounced around in the back of the pick-up along the stony road out of Aghios Kirikos. In a way, I considered it to be a free delivery, but in reality it had cost me a small fortune.

As we carried the mattress to the house, Jim said, 'You want a bed for this? I bring you one from my grandmother.'

🖂

It was after midnight and I sat on the quayside waiting for the potato boat from Samos to dock. Stelios had rung me at the taverna telling me a man called Manos would pay me five hundred drachma if I could unload it in four hours. All I had to do was chuck all the sacks onto the back of a lorry and the job was done. Whenever anyone told me a job was going to be simple and I could make easy money, it always put me on edge.

Manos was late, and there was no sign of a boat coming into the harbour. I didn't doubt that Manos would eventually arrive; he was, after all, behaving like an Ikarian. And apparently he was Stelios's cousin, although everybody seemed to be everyone's cousin, further entangling the branches on the Ikarian ancestral tree. Such things go on in your mind when you're sitting around waiting for someone.

I wasn't only up for the job because of the money: I liked working through the night when no one was around. I felt closer to the natural world after all the noise had subsided. Which it would eventually, though I could still hear music coming from the cafés in the market place. For the Ikarians the night was young, families still parading around under the sycamore trees.

Manos was of heavy stock, with muscular arms and large thighs that bulged against his tight-fitting jeans. He walked at ten to two, I believe is the expression, his feet sticking out at an angle. He had broad shoulders and was wearing a T-shirt that didn't quite reach his trousers, exposing a belly button that reminded me of a front door bell. He knew who I was, of course, and greeted me with a handshake that nearly dislocated my elbow.

As he was explaining to me in reasonable English what he wanted me to do, a lorry reversed up behind us, and at the same time the boat, a little larger than Stelios's, spluttered its way into the harbour. It was weighed down with sacks of potatoes, piled high all over the deck. As I had feared, I could see my five hundred drachma would be hard earned. These were not twenty-five kilo bags. They looked more like fifty.

The lorry driver, a man of considerable years with only a few remaining strands of grey wispy hair, was going to help me with the sacks and then drive them to a warehouse somewhere.

After giving his instructions, Manos was gone and the bearded skipper, who obviously had only one thing on his mind, opened a bottle of ouzo, leant back against the cabin and slowly got drunk.

The lorry driver, Adonis, who sadly no longer lived up to his name, then gave me a full description of the tactics to be employed. He was clearly a man of vast experience in all things to do with unloading potatoes. He knew only individual words of English, not sentences, but they were words packed with essential meaning, like ballbreaker, heart attack and bloody heavy. He illustrated perfectly with a series of graceful hand movements that the rise and fall of the vessel made timing the delivery of each sack critical. I had to have it over my shoulder as the boat rose up, enabling me to slide it on to the quayside. Adonis would then shove a trolley under it and run it up a ramp to tip it neatly into the back of the lorry.

So began a night of working as a co-ordinated duo, rhythmically rising and falling with the movement of the sea. At times it was almost balletic, and we only occasionally got out of step with each other, and no doubt Torvill and Dean did too. We worked hard on our timing and soon corrected ourselves, Adonis being in exactly the right place as I came up with another sack. I thought we could speed everything up if Adonis put the trolley closer to the harbour edge, then I could throw a sack straight on to it, but it was hardly the time to change the system now. Adonis might have thought I was a bit of a know-all.

It was four thirty when we got the last sack on to the lorry, by which time the skipper was snoring loudly, slumped over the now empty bottle of ouzo. Adonis and I had taken to each other, not that we said anything, but we both knew we had enjoyed working together. Maybe he shouldn't have, but he cut open one of the sacks and put some potatoes in a bag for me and then drove off down the quayside into the breaking light of a new day. As for me, I walked back to Lefkada, exhausted but satisfied with the night's work.

5.

It was Seth's birthday. He was three years old, and I could honestly say that, so far, he had ambled through life. Although Sam and Lysta had built up the arrival of his big day and we all stood over his bed and sang it to him, he denied it.

'It's tomorrow,' he said and seemed quite annoyed, as if he had something else planned for the day.

A lot of thought had gone into what we were going to give him. We wanted him to have only things that would occupy him through the months to come. Ros couldn't bear it when children discarded their presents the very day after receiving them. Sam and Lysta gave him a butterfly net and a pencil case. And from Ros and me he had a magnifying glass. We were sure Seth would enjoy these gifts, and we were right. Being only three foot tall and close to the earth, he spent most of his time lost in a world of little scampering treats. He already had a cardboard box next to his bed full of dead insects which he could now empty out and study in the finest detail. Once he got the hang of the magnifying glass he spent most of his birthday on his hands and knees looking at everything that moved, and a lot that didn't.

Maria brought out a most unusual cake with a plastic donkey stuck on the top of it and what appeared to be two wise men sunk into the icing; obviously old Christmas decorations. She had to light its three candles several times, because the breeze kept blowing them out.

In the taverna that night Seth sat holding a jam jar with a grasshopper in it. I told him it needed air and would die if he didn't undo the lid, which he did, but unfortunately it hopped out. Armed with the magnifying glass he crawled under the tables, returning without the grasshopper but with a spider instead, for which he crumbled up dry eucalyptus leaves as a tasty treat. After that he'd had enough of his birthday, and fell asleep for twelve hours.

⌗

It never ceased to surprise me who worked with whom on Ikaria, how families were connected, what financial arrangements were in place. Why, for instance, was Stamati delivering trays of baklava to Maria? He pulled up outside the taverna squashed into the cab of a Daihatsu three-wheeler, the engine sounding like an over-revved lawn mower, still wearing his apron. He kissed me on each cheek, playing the injured soul, saying that I had neglected him.

'You have no use for me now.'

I wasn't going to respond to that. Yannis helped him carry the trays into the kitchen while Maria sat at one of the tables counting out the drachma. Stamati stuck the money into his trouser pocket and offered to buy me an Amstel, a Dutch beer which had become my favourite drink now the days were hotter. It was cold and refreshing, unlike retsina, which dried your mouth out.

It was pure chance that I should be sitting there with Stamati, but he didn't hold back in voicing his opinion about my activities on the island.

'You are a fool to work with Jim. Anybody will tell you that; the man has no money. And now you work in the monastery. The sister is without friends and what will you get from her? Food for the family, nothing else.'

There was no point in asking how he knew all this, because everyone knew everything. He was so condemning that it made me wonder why he should feel so strongly about it. Why did he always show such interest in me?

'Stelios pays me, but I could do with more work,' I said.

'Yes, and who brought you Stelios . . . me, yes?'

Well, that was true, but what was Stamati's point? Why was he so concerned?

'And I will tell you something as well. Jim's brother, he will be trouble for you.'

'What do you mean?'

'You think he will pay you when he sees the work on his house?' he said, with a sarcastic laugh. 'You can work with me in the restaurant . . . serve at the tables, yes, and I give you more money and you will be happy.'

'Thank you, Stamati, but I couldn't work in a restaurant. I need to be outside, and I'm no waiter.'

He swallowed the last dregs of his Amstel and wiped the froth from his lips.

'Will you come and see my mother? She is old, she is sad. Come and tell her of your life in Wales . . . yes, you must promise me this.'

With that, he stood up, went over to pay Maria for the beers, and left.

I went back to the house. Ros was making a Greek salad on the terrace with Lysta beside her, intently reading out loud Enid Blyton's *Five Go Off to Camp*. I started to tell Ros what had happened, but didn't get very far.

'Dad, that's rude. I was in the middle of a sentence.'

'I'm sorry, but I have to talk to Mum for a minute. Ros, what is it about Stamati? I find all the attention he's giving me quite peculiar. Now he's offered me a job.'

Ros's reaction was an amused smile that gradually crept across her face and she looked at me sweetly; her hands smelled of onion when she caressed my cheek. What had I done to deserve this?

'You know I wouldn't have you any other way, but you really are quite naïve.'

'What do you mean?'

'I noticed it the first week we were here. He's lonely, he likes you, he lives with his mother.'

'I don't understand . . . are you saying he fancies me?'

'Yes, that's exactly what I'm saying. Asking you to be a waiter in his restaurant! Whatever next?'

'Mum, can I carry on reading now?'

'I wouldn't encourage him if I were you.'

'He's already kissed me on both cheeks.'

'Dad, you're being silly. Men don't kiss each other.'

Sam appeared then, struggling up the steps with a heavy bag.

'Mum, if I peel these apples for Maria, she's going to give me a vanilla paste.'

Lysta continued with *Five Go Off to Camp*, and I left to go to the monastery to milk the goats. Ros told me to be wary of one of them that she thought had come into season and had head-butted her between the legs.

'Painful,' I said.

'Not as painful as it would be for you.'

'I'll roll up a T-shirt and stick it down my trousers.'

'Good idea.'

7

The Kidnappers

We had moved into our new house. Although we'd left all the windows open, we should have waited another couple of days: everywhere smelled of paint. Maria's cousin, who lived over in Raches, was so delighted with what we'd done that he'd furnished it for us. We now had a chest of drawers, chairs and a kitchen table. He also gave us three beds for the children and it was still rent free.

Datsun Jim had given us what was originally his grandmother's bed, which he delivered, together with its long history. Apparently six children had been born in it and his grandfather had died in it before it was lent to his mother, who carried on the family tradition, giving birth to another five children and yes, finally, Datsun Jim, who emerged into the world in this bed. Made of iron, which was just as well, it looked in remarkably good condition considering its eventful past, but then I suppose every bed could tell a story. It was quite rigid once it was slotted together, and on all four corners brass knobs glowed in the sunlight. Our mattress fitted perfectly. At last we might look forward to a good night's sleep.

But, as always with Jim, nothing was simple. His grandmother hadn't actually given us the bed. She was ninety-two years old and had a habit of forgetting things and then remembering them. So the bed was on loan, and if she realised it was missing we would have to return it.

'Where does your grandmother sleep now?' Ros asked.

'She is happy with a single bed at her age.'

We said we couldn't possibly take it, but he was adamant and insisted. Ros thought he was trying to show himself in a better light. His brother was expected back any day now, and at long last I might get paid.

🔄

I described Stelios in a letter to my mother as a man who was a law unto himself, who never rehearsed for the day that lay ahead, because the only thing that was predictable was the unexpected. He was naturally extrovert and had already shown me he wasn't averse to taking risks. He was larger than life and there was an invincibility about him.

So when I found him sitting cross-legged mending the nets, which always had gaping holes in them, I wondered what had happened. He was usually glad to see me, impatient to be off, but now he looked bedraggled and seemed subdued and withdrawn. The Karelia stuck in the corner of his mouth had nearly burnt down to the filter. There was no sparkle in his face today, and the calm Aegean was clearly doing nothing to lift his inner gloom.

Out at sea, with the sun high above, the light refracted in the clear water, I could see shoals of fish zigzagging beneath us, their silver scales sparkling like jewels, no more than two feet below the surface, but Stelios didn't say a word. Only when the nets were down and we lounged on the deck did we talk. He threw me an old denim cap, telling me to put it on so the sun didn't burn my head.

'I am a quiet man today,' he said, scooping up a handful of water and washing his face.

'You have no words in you,' I said.

'Oh, I do . . . but not to speak.'

'Not even one?'

'Ha! I have one, no, two . . . bloody women!'

When the day's fishing was done and we returned to Aghios

Kirikos he ought to have been a happier man, for the catch was the biggest I'd seen since we had been fishing together. We set out at least a dozen boxes of fish on the quayside and almost immediately a kind of chaotic auction took place. I had no idea how anybody understood what was going on, but then I couldn't in the cattle market back in Bryncir, where everything was sold to a buyer who raised an eyebrow at the right time. It was the same here: a lot of fast talking, with the highest bidder kicking away his box of fish and slapping the auctioneer's hand. When the deal was done and the money counted out, young boys out to earn a few drachma rushed in and carried the boxes away. These buyers must have been restaurant owners because I saw Stamati amongst them, bidding in the mêlée.

When it was over and Stelios gave me my usual bag of fish, I knew there was no room in Maria's fridge for the octopus and squid. Perhaps I could sell them to Stamati, who was walking ahead of me empty-handed, pretending not to know I was there.

'Hey, Stamati, you haven't any fish.'

'The price is too much for me.'

'I have some octopus and squid if you're interested.'

'So this is why you talk to me.'

I ignored that. 'How much will you give me?'

'Because you treat me badly, no more than a hundred and fifty,' he said, looking into the bag. He knew a good deal when he saw one.

⑤

When Lysta said that she wanted to do the shopping for us in Aghios Kirikos, my first reaction was an absolute no. Not after what had happened to Sam. But she put up a good argument as to why she should be allowed to prove herself.

'He's only five minutes older than me, and you said boys don't mature as quickly as girls. It's not fair.'

I did remember saying that, but I made her promise that she wouldn't get into anyone's car and would come straight home. At least she was less likely than Sam to be tempted by a large lunch and football on the beach.

It was a Saturday, which meant nothing at all; every day on Ikaria was the same, except the children didn't go to school at the weekend. It was nearly the end of June, and not unusual for the temperature to be up in the eighties.

Whilst Lysta went shopping the rest of us went to the beach, less than a five-minute walk from Lefkada. As we passed the taverna, Maria ran out and grabbed me by the arm and pulled me into the kitchen. She opened the fridge and showed me the small freezer compartment, which was full of octopus and squid again.

'Yours,' she said, pointing at me. 'No good.'

We were still not eating through the catch, which wasn't surprising as no one except me liked octopus or squid, and I'd had enough of eating them every day. So she suggested as it was Saturday, and because some Greek-American families were now back on the island, she'd use them in a traditional meal that night.

'No more in my fridge. You understand?'

I realised I might have reached the point when another squid would be a squid too far, and the last thing I wanted to do was upset Maria. We had grown fond of her and Yannis. It felt as if they had adopted us, and they often gave the children their favourite vanilla drink, waving away payment.

We ate at the taverna every night, something that would have been beyond our pocket if the barbunia I gave Maria hadn't been popular with everyone, so that she was reluctant to charge us for meals. If I asked Yannis how much I owed him, he just said, '*Avrio*.' So we slipped into this unspoken arrangement. I just hoped that if they thought we owed them anything, Yannis would put a bill on the table. We spent more time at the taverna than we did at home; what with the people we met there and the long evenings, it felt as if we only went back to the house to sleep.

Ros, Sam and Seth were already stripped down to their swimming costumes when I caught up with them. The small sandy beach was no more than five yards below the coastal road, protected from the wind by a jutting peninsula of dark rocks.

'Ros, I think this might be a good time to bring up the delicate subject of my swimming trunks.' It was an annual occurrence and usually took place on a beach.

'I know what you're going to say,' she said, resigned to the fact that the matter had to be discussed. 'I really don't know why I haven't,' she added, squirting the last of the Ambre Solaire on to Sam's and Seth's pink bodies.

'It doesn't matter. I'll do what I always do, swim in my shorts.'

This all went back to when Ros threw out a pair of hideously tight-fitting swimming trunks that she had bought for me at a jumble sale. They were too obscene to describe, but I had dared to wear them on Harlech beach on a rare hot day in Wales and I ran into the sea in front of a crowd of spectators. She'd covered her face in embarrassment and told me later that her girlfriends couldn't understand what she saw in me. She had promised to buy me a new pair that would give me a less controversial look.

That was three years ago. So now I swam in a pair of baggy shorts, held up by a belt. Not the most attractive beachwear, but not bad enough for Ros to do anything about it.

We were the only ones on the beach that morning, enjoying

the crystal-clear waters of the Aegean. The Ikarians preferred to swim after their siesta. It had become an interesting pastime to watch the various ways the locals entered the sea. Middle-aged women rarely went in alone, preferring to brave the water in the company of a friend. Under wide-brimmed straw hats, they talked incessantly, and only ever walked in up to their waists. Sometimes when a wave rushed in they rose up together, like synchronised bobbing sea birds, keeping their plumage dry. They never submerged themselves, or swam a single stroke. When they came out they strolled up and down the shoreline, still engrossed in their chatter.

One who sought attention was a silver-haired man in his early sixties. Suntanned and muscled up, he ran into the water without hesitation, like an athlete, and dived over the incoming waves, breaking into the crawl. With the style of an Olympic swimmer, he was far from the shore in seconds; even the way he breathed between each stroke looked professional. As he walked from the sea he swept his hair back, exuding a virile self-awareness. He also put on a show drying himself, adjusting his black trunks so his manhood was centrally positioned. He finished off this little performance by doing a few press-ups, then lay face down on his towel. The act was the same every time he came to the beach.

'If he's still got it, let him flaunt it,' said Ros. 'What's wrong with having pride in your body?' she added, suggesting I might be a little jealous.

'Me jealous? Watch this.' And I did twenty press-ups there and then.

'I must say, you are pretty fit. And not an ounce of fat on you.'

'Fancy me, do you?'

'I've never stopped.'

'Feel that,' I said, tightening my biceps.

'You're a Greek god with an English accent, but you'll do for me.'

'*Efkharisto*, baby.'

We went home for lunch, thinking Lysta should be back soon. In fact, she had already returned and had left two bags of shopping on the kitchen table, with a note: *I've gone to look for you.*

'Why don't you go and find her while I make lunch,' said Ros.

I asked Maria if she had seen her, which she had, half an hour earlier, carrying the shopping. She must have headed off again in the other direction, which was strange, as she knew which beach we always went to.

So we decided to eat, convinced Lysta would turn up in a few minutes. She didn't, and those anxieties that come when a child has not returned rolled in again. So I walked up the road towards the monastery, and fifteen minutes later saw a car I recognised, the red Fiat I had dragged Sam from, parked by the roadside. They were on the beach, the whole family having a picnic, Lysta amongst them. I didn't rush down and join them; I could see Lysta was enjoying herself. I decided to take the cold, unfriendly approach, controlled but aloof.

'Dad, Dad!' shouted Lysta, waving at me, but I ignored her. I stared straight at the father, who was lying on the sand, eating a hard-boiled egg.

'Will you please stop kidnapping my children,' I said. 'I'm fed up with it.'

He immediately got to his feet, offering me a handshake and a huge smile. It did nothing to soften my mood.

'I'm Vassili, and please this is my wife Agathi, and my children, Christos, Xenia and Leftari.'

'You speak good English, so you will understand that I am angry. You must stop running off with my children.'

They looked at me in astonishment.

Lysta didn't back me up in my role of the angry father.

'You should have left a note on the door. No one was at home so I went looking for you. Where were you, Dad?' She told me she had got back with the shopping in under two hours and I should have been pleased with her. I felt slightly on the wrong foot.

Agathi came forward. With a pleading look in her eyes, she said, 'We are not a bad family. We saw Lysta on the road, that is all, and asked her to have lunch with us.'

'Dad, I've made friends with Xenia. We're the same age.' What else could I do? I apologised, although it didn't feel quite right after the anxiety they had put us through. But when they asked me to join them I could hardly refuse, and after a few minutes I relaxed and began to enjoy their company.

Agathi had the strong features that many Greek women have: high cheekbones and dark eyes. She had a beautiful mouth and black, shoulder-length hair. She taught English, her second language, at the primary school in Aghios Kirikos, which reminded me that Lysta and I needed to get back to Ros. Such was the impression the whole family had made by then, I suggested we should all meet again soon and have a picnic on the beach.

🔂

The hot springs in the village of Therma, a fifteen-minute walk the other side of Aghios Kirikos, had been known since ancient times. I knew of no other place on Ikaria that was promoted as a tourist attraction, with entrance fees and towels provided.

Only local people knew that below Lefkada there were also thermal springs that bubbled up to the surface of the Aegean. A hidden, overgrown track through the low scrub of thyme and gnarled bushes that could have been made by goats led to a steep slope down to the rocky shore. This was no easy descent, with obstacles every few yards, such as tree roots, overhanging branches, and loose scree that made you lose your footing. Once by the sea you had to pick your way from rock to rock for a few hundred yards to a small promontory. There you would see the first evidence of the springs – a slight steam rising. Entering the water required great care, because the temperature varied dramatically and in places was scalding. Maria had bathed there for years, but not any longer, the trek now being too arduous for her. She might have been getting on, but her skin always had a healthy sheen. Whether it was because of the hot springs or all the olive oil that she also swore by I didn't know.

One morning I went down to the springs myself, not that I was seeking a miraculous cure. I set off early, when the day was cool, and even at my age it took some time to get there. Every step had to be taken with the utmost care, especially when leaping across a landscape of slippery boulders. If you were nimble enough to survive the hazards it was highly likely you would have the place to yourself. The fact that the location of the springs had remained a secret and they were so difficult to get to showed the Ikarians' complete lack of interest in exploiting their island for tourism.

But that morning when I eventually reached the springs, I found myself not alone but in the company of Icarus, who claimed to be ninety years old. He was frail and skeletal, with no more than a few strands of white hair and a suntan that you could tell would never fade. He had spent most of his life in the merchant navy, had seen the world and spoke good English. I couldn't believe he'd walked here, and then I saw the rubber dinghy drifting nearby on a long rope.

When I introduced myself and told him what I was doing

on Ikaria he opened up about life on the island. I wanted to find out what kept him going. Surely at that age everything was a tremendous effort? I had never met someone so old, and with such enthusiasm for the things he still enjoyed.

'The stillness of clear mornings, the sea air, to float in the Aegean.'

'Is that all? Is that the secret of old age?'

'Yes, although some say too that Ikarians have little stress in their lives because they don't pursue material riches.'

'And the hot springs, do they possess the healing qualities everybody claims?'

'Well, look at me. If I stood up you could watch me bend down and touch my toes.'

Which he did when we parted, and then with a single oar paddled away in the dinghy, ghost-like, as if he was disappearing back into ancient myth.

🖼️

On an island with a complete disregard for time, Sister Ulita had discovered a game that gave her a childish delight. Ironically it was to do with punctuality, because in the mornings I was never late. She would wait behind the monastery gate, counting down the seconds until I rang the bell, and as soon as I did she would pull it open with such ferocity that the birds in the courtyard flew into the trees, not returning until the reverberating metallic hum had faded away. I always pretended to be taken completely by surprise, which delighted her even more. She did it every morning, no matter whether it was me or Ros, then clapped her hands to chase away the solitary chicken that was always escaping from the run.

Ros told me that Sister Ulita's routine didn't always follow the strict discipline of her holy orders when the children were at the monastery. She gave them lessons which required no words, showing them how to make yoghurt and cheese, which in anyone's language is educational. Once Ros had milked the goats and poured the milk through a sieve into the jugs that had been set out for her in the kitchen, the only thing left to do was to tether the goats on a fresh spot of land in the shade of the olive trees. Then Sister Ulita's divine obedience showed a little flexibility, usually in the form of a ball which she would hit into the air with a tennis racket, hoping Sam and Lysta would catch it. These games rarely lasted more than a few minutes before the ball disappeared over the monastery wall.

This was all done in the hope of delaying their departure. It made me wonder what satisfaction the nun gained from living such a solitary life, cut off from the world, hidden away behind the monastery's high walls and her impenetrable sunglasses, showing only a smile and those white teeth.

🔳

I'd hardly been living in some remote rainforest, but when Lottie arrived at the taverna, looking worn out, dragging a heavy suitcase from the back of a farmer's three-wheeled truck, it reminded me that life beyond Ikaria still existed. She had come from a world I had completely lost touch with, hence my curiosity, which she must have found quite off-putting. I had gleaned little news of what was happening on planet earth, not even who had won this year's FA Cup.

Lottie was Dutch, in her early twenties, wearing a short black sleeveless dress. Her long blonde hair swished from side to side as she walked. I think she thought I was the waiter showing her to a table.

'I don't work here,' I said, sitting down with her.

'You behave as though you do,' she smiled. Like most of the

Dutch she spoke perfect English, with that soft seductive burr that draws you to them.

'Neither do I work for the Ikarian tourist board,' I said 'which doesn't exist anyway. But welcome to Lefkada. I'm Nikko, if you want to call me by my Greek name. Let me find Maria for you.'

'Can you get me an Amstel, an ice cold one, in a frozen glass? I haven't slept for twenty-four hours and I need to revive myself.'

'Of course. Do you want something to eat?'

'What have they got?'

'Squid and octopus,' I said, hoping to tempt her, 'beautifully cooked in olive oil, which by the way I caught myself.'

'You're a fisherman!'

'Amongst other things: gardener, house builder, whatever comes along.'

'I'll just have the beer and a few olives.'

I was hungry for a good conversation, starved these past months of a flow of words that I didn't have to decipher. It was easy on the ear listening to her, despite being surrounded by the incessant thrum of the cicadas.

'Doesn't that noise get on your nerves? Is it like that all the time?'

'I promise you, in a couple of days you won't notice it. Why have you come to Lefkada?' I asked.

'They told me in Aghios Kirikos there's a good beach here where I can pitch a tent.'

'How long will you stay?'

'Who knows? Let's see what happens,' she said, watching Maria pour out a cold beer. Then, gradually tilting her glass, she swallowed the lot. 'And what brings you here?' So I told her about the vagaries of fate, arriving in Piraeus and getting on the first boat, which happened to be coming to Ikaria.

For her it was running from the bitter experience of a broken heart, which I skipped over, not wanting to open wounds she was trying to heal. I wanted to know what was going on in the world.

'All the same stuff: too many cars, pollution, wars, everyone living on the edge. Believe me, you are better off here,' she said emphatically. 'Look, my take on life isn't that positive at the moment. I'm sure if you talk to someone else you'll hear a completely different story.'

And I did. Less than an hour later Gregory turned up at the taverna. A Canadian from Montreal, with a mass of blond curls and an expensive camera around his neck, he was outgoing and upbeat. He seemed a gregarious young man who said everything was groovy. I introduced him to Lottie.

'Hey, didn't I see you on the ferry last night, trying to balance some glasses of beer on a tray?'

'Yes, that was me. It was fine until the boat suddenly rolled.'

'I suppose it could have been worse,' said Gregory, smiling.

'What happened?' I asked.

'Well, from what I saw, there were two priests and a woman involved.'

'Yes, she was an opera singer,' said Lottie regretfully. 'Soaked, I'm afraid.'

'It was quite a scene for a while,' said Gregory enthusiastically.

'It was embarrassing for me. She is singing tonight in Samos . . . I hope she has recovered.'

Sitting in their company, it felt as if the summer season had begun. Visitors arriving. I was excited by the thought of it. It was only now I realised what stimulation new people bring to life on an island.

It was late afternoon when I left Gregory and Lottie over their beers to join Ros and the children on the beach. I was about to take the path down from the road when Datsun Jim pulled up in front of me. He was panicking and could hardly get his words out. He took deep breaths in a cloud of dust. He spat, then blew his nose into that dirty handkerchief. It all seemed to be leading up to something pretty dramatic.

'Giorgos,' he said at last.

'Yes, what about Giorgos? Has he brought me my money?' I asked.

'He is angry . . . very angry, about the house.'

'I'm sure he is, but what has that got to do with me?'

'It is the mess, and all the cement that is wasted.'

Again I asked him what it had to do with me.

'He is coming to the taverna tomorrow night.'

'Good. At last I will be paid.'

'You do not understand. He is angry.'

'Yes I do, Jim. I understand he is angry, but with you, not with me.'

🔁

We met Agathi and Vassili for the promised picnic. I knew Ros and Agathi would like each other, sitting on the beach, watching their children playing together. You could say they were both schoolteachers, Ros now taking her role so seriously that every evening she prepared Sam and Lysta's lessons for the next day. The kitchen walls were gradually being covered by their school work, mostly Seth's abstract watercolours that looked like the beginning of the universe.

'Agathi is lovely; we have so much in common. And she's going to give us a blackboard and chalk. It really has been a wonderful day.' One of those great ironies, how everything can give way to its opposite. Suddenly the kidnappers had become our new best friends.

'I've met some new friends as well. Why don't you come to the taverna and meet them?'

'Dad, can I ask you something?' said Sam, wearing the deep, concentrated look that meant he was about to deliver one of life's perplexing conundrums.

'Do I need to sit down for it?' I asked him.

'Yes, I think you do.'

We each pulled up a chair and sat on the terrace.

'OK, let's hear it.'

'Why has Christos got a different willy to mine?'

'Oh . . . that's a good one. Well, I'm going to have to use a very long word.'

'Shall I get the notebook I'm writing all my new words in?'

'That's a good idea.'

When he returned, pencil poised, he looked across at me expectantly. 'Tell me what it is.'

So I slowly spelt out circumcision, which he wrote down in capital letters.

'What does it mean?'

Just as I was about to try to explain, Ros came out of the house and said, 'Shall we go over to the taverna now?'

'We'll join you later,' I replied. 'I think we might be some time.'

8

The Arm Wrestler

I told Ros I was going to sleep under the stars that night. I knew the exact spot, just above the house where the land rose high enough to be able to see the Aegean and, with my head propped up on my coat as a pillow, I could gaze at the sky. I had once spent a night on Salisbury Plain with an eccentric boffin with a Heath Robinson telescope who convinced me that it was only a matter of time before someone out there contacted us. I lost touch with him when he upped sticks and went to live on an uninhabited island off the Australian coast that he called World's End. There isn't anywhere bigger than space and I was hoping I might witness some cosmic activity, maybe even something more than a shooting star.

When Sam got wind of what I was planning, he said he wanted to come too. I couldn't say no; after all, I had already filled his head with the possibility that we were not alone in the universe. He wanted to bring his notebook and keep a record of everything we saw, and to have a picnic at midnight.

He got more and more excited as darkness fell. I told him I wasn't going until at least eleven o'clock, way past his bedtime, but he said if he fell asleep I was to wake him up. At half past nine he was still going strong so we went down to the taverna where Maria was welcoming two girls with rucksacks on their backs. A few people had been turning up in the past couple of weeks, but none had stayed more than a night or two, pitching their tents on the beach and then disappearing. I never really met them because they only came to the taverna to take water from the standpipe. They cooked food on the fires they lit on the beach and had their own scene going on down there. Only Gregory and Lottie came up and spent time at the taverna.

I thought Maria was telling the newcomers where they would find this group of backpackers, but she called me over to meet them.

'They are English,' she said.

The look a person greets you with shows so much, before a word is spoken. With shoulder-length dark brown hair these two could have been sisters, but they weren't. They both shook my hand with a warmth that drew me in.

'I'm Julia. I'm a Kiwi, actually,' which you could tell immediately from her accent.

'I'm Sarah, and I'm English.'

'So am I. I'm Nick and this is my son, Sam.'

'Hello. I am half Welsh and half English.'

'Which half of you is English?' asked Julia.

'The top half, I think. In my head I support Spurs, don't I, Dad?'

They'd just arrived from Naxos and didn't know how long they would stay. In their late teens or early twenties, they were well tanned, their packs sun-bleached and their sandals dusty; clearly they'd been in the islands for a while. Maria had already offered them a room in the house above the taverna, where she hung her cheeses in muslin bags.

'We'll meet properly tomorrow,' I said. 'Tonight Sam and I are sleeping under the stars.'

It didn't turn out to be the night I had been hoping for, silently contemplating the starry heavens. Not that Sam got bored. In fact, his imagination took over and within the first half an hour he had already spotted three UFOs, one of which was on fire and had crashed into the sea.

'There, Dad, over there! You missed it again!'

He did eventually fall asleep on a sleeping bag and I pulled another one over him. It was a warm, moonless night, all the better for seeing the stars. Nearby I could hear wild goats bleating as they munched the scrub. But by one o'clock I was done with stargazing; beautiful as the night sky might be, there wasn't a lot going on. I knew I wouldn't fall asleep. For a start, I couldn't get comfortable; the ground was hard and uneven. Then I felt hungry and decided to eat our picnic, bread and cheese, which I washed down with an Amstel.

After that I made my way back to the house, carrying Sam asleep in my arms, where I could enjoy the rest of the night tucked up next to Ros. In the morning, when he woke to find himself mysteriously back in his own bed, Sam shook me awake, wondering what had happened. It was as if the intervening hours had not existed, and he continued the conversation we were having before he fell asleep.

'Dad, if we're not alone and the aliens don't speak English . . .'

'Yes, what's your point?' I said, trying to wake myself up.

'What are we going to say to each other?'

'I think that's the first question you've asked that no one has the answer to.'

' "Can we be friends?" is what I'd say.'

'That's a good first line.'

🔲

I spent hours at the monastery, usually on my own, digging the soil under a blazing sun. Often I'd take off my T-shirt and work half naked, but only when I was sure Sister Ulita wasn't around. In the same way, I'd sometimes smoke a quiet cigarette, one eye on the watch for her. Although I worked hard and deserved breaks, I wasn't sure whether smoking in the monastery grounds contravened any of her laws.

It was another hot afternoon. I was hoeing the weeds between the pepper plants, lost in my own thoughts, and hadn't noticed her coming into the garden. She shouted, 'Neeko, Neeko,' clearly agitated, turning her face away and wagging a finger. I stopped hoeing and put my T-shirt back on.

'If I can't take off my shirt, I will only dig early in the morning,' I said, even though I knew she couldn't understand what I was saying. It was a moment when we suddenly felt an awkward tension between us and she left the garden.

A few minutes later she brought me some water, as if to make amends, and wouldn't leave until I had emptied the glass. She smiled then, saying, '*Poli zesti*,' playfully flicking water droplets at my face, almost as if she was sprinkling me with holy water. I wished she would take off her sunglasses; it was frustrating not being able to see her eyes.

After I'd milked the goats and taken the bucket into the old stone pantry, I helped Sister Ulita fill the basket on the front of her moped with eggs, which I passed to her one by one until she had packed them all, without any protection whatsoever. She obviously knew what she was doing, or maybe there was a knack to it, because they were quite rigid and didn't move an inch. Then she fired up the moped and sped out through the monastery gates. I thought I had witnessed one of life's great mysteries; surely they would all end up smashed.

When I got back to Lefkada, Julia and Sarah were in the taverna. Julia was washing her hair, bending down under the standpipe, wearing a sarong. You had to be pretty supple to get into the various positions required to wash away the shampoo. Sarah was drinking coffee at a table nearby. I noticed that her auburn hair had been lightened by the sun and she had striking blue eyes.

'So, whereabouts in England are you from?' I asked.

She told me she had grown up on a dairy farm in Sussex; not yet nineteen, she was going to Exeter University in September to read English and philosophy. In just five minutes of conversation, I realised how much we had in common. I was a country boy, born and bred in Dorset. There was an Englishness about her I felt at home with; nothing I could articulate, just a feeling of ease in her company. Julia came over and joined us, her hair wrapped up in a towel like a turban.

'How did you two meet?'

'Absolute chance, really,' said Julia. 'I was staying on my aunt's yacht in St Katharine's Dock at Tower Bridge.'

'And I was working nearby at the Cruising Association. We got chatting and soon found we both wanted to go to Greece.'

'A few weeks later we were on the Magic Bus to Athens. A long uncomfortable journey we endured together.'

'Yes, that's how we got here – baptism by fire!' I said.

'By the way,' asked Julia, 'do you know where they're holding the next *panagiri*? We want to dance the night away to Greek music.'

I suggested they talk to Maria, that she would know. We hadn't been to one, but I'd heard these festivals happened from time to time, mostly in remote villages in the hills.

Ros and the children came down to sit with us.

As we listened to Julia telling us about the wild, wonderful landscape of New Zealand, Sam, with the faraway look of someone lost in his own thoughts, asked, 'Why do you speak English in such a funny way?'

'That's my accent. Don't you like it?'

'Yes, it's just different.'

'Well, so is yours.'

'What's the longest word in New Zealand?' asked Sam, opening his notebook.

'The words are all the same as you have in England, except, of course, the Maori ones, like *pohutukawa*.'

'Wow, what's that?'

'It's the New Zealand Christmas tree.'

'That's really good. But I'm looking for the longest word in the world.'

'If you want an extremely long word, Sam,' said Ros, 'there's a Welsh town called Llanfairpwllgwyngyllgogerychwyrndrobwllllantysiliogogogoch. It's very near where we used to live.'

'God, Mum, that's silly. There wouldn't be enough room to write it on an envelope. How many letters is it?'

'I think it's about fifty.'

'Is it the longest word in the world?'

'I wouldn't be surprised.'

Maria called me into the kitchen. The telephone had rung and it was Stelios.

'Hey, you come tomorrow? Theo will be with us.'

'OK, what time?'

'Six o'clock. Don't be late.'

When I told Julia and Sarah I was going fishing the next day, they were keen to go too. I wasn't sure.

'Come to Aghios in the morning and let's see what Stelios says.'

Gregory the Gregarious, as I called him, joined us then, up from the beach. What better place to be than sitting in the taverna exchanging ideas in the long summer nights, having a stimulating debate? But I'd decided tonight I wouldn't drink retsina because I had a feeling it made me babble on, and Ros had said she would share a carafe of the less alcoholic Ikarian red wine which Maria was always wanting me to try.

I told Gregory he had the look of an ancient Greek. Although he was only twenty-five, he would not have been out of place dining in the Acropolis, wearing a white robe, drinking wine from a goblet.

'Yes, reclining on a chaise longue,' said Julia.

'And your concubine tempting you with a bunch of grapes,' added Sarah.

'Unless my history is completely screwed up, I don't think you'd find a chaise longue in the Acropolis,' Lottie said as she joined us.

'What's your bloodline, Gregory?' I continued. 'Have you ever traced it back?'

'Well with a name like Van Brinker you would think my ancestors were Dutch.'

'Logical thinking,' I said. 'So you're more comfortable in clogs than sandals.'

'No, I'm more comfortable in sandals.'

'There we have the clue,' I said.

'You mean my preference in footwear can be traced back to the ancient Greeks?'

'It could be. I think we should keep an open mind about it.'

The place was full, which meant Maria was busy in the kitchen, and whenever Yannis was the waiter service was more than a little haphazard. He still believed he could memorise the menu, and not writing down the orders didn't help. Often we were given someone else's meal, and it was quicker to walk round the tables to find the people who'd ordered it than to get him to sort it out. Nobody complained; they all felt sorry for him.

I had already spoken to Maria so there was every chance we would get the squid and octopus, which Gregory and Lottie wanted to try. Everyone at the taverna that night eventually ate a meal, although whether it was what they'd expected was another matter. But Gregory and Lottie did get their order and enjoyed it, which was all I really cared about, and Sarah and Julia had some too. Not that they had ordered it.

At dawn I went down to the taverna where the two girls were already waiting for me, both disturbed by what they had found lurking in one of Sarah's sandals. Still half asleep and about to put her foot on it, she had seen the scorpion just in time. I thought I'd heard a scream while I was dressing. She had carefully picked up the sandal and carried it outside, tipped the scorpion on to the grass and watched it crawl away.

'Are you nervous about sleeping there now?' I asked.

'No, but maybe we need a torch to check the room before we go to bed. I can't believe how close I was to being stung,' she said, still clearly shaken.

We met Stelios on the quayside and he was happy for them to come out with us. Julia wasn't really dressed for a day's fishing; the wind had steadily increased as we'd walked from Lefkada and she had to keep holding down her light, sleeveless dress. Sarah had no such problems, since she was wearing a pair of denim shorts.

'Of course, come,' he said. I could tell by the way he looked at them that he had an eye for the girls. Then he introduced us to a slim young man with boyish looks who was at that sensitive age when boys grow facial fluff rather than dark stubble. His thick hair was swept back off his forehead.

'This is my brother Theo.'

'*Yassas*,' Theo said in greeting, jumping on board and then offering Julia and Sarah a helping hand. He was not at all as I had imagined. He was taller than Stelios and quietly spoken, as if unsure of himself in front of people he didn't know.

Stelios called me down into the cabin, 'You know, I have as you say to change my tactics.'

'What do you mean?' I said.

'My mother, she says I bully him,' which, from what he had told me, was probably the case. 'So I am glad you bring the girls today. You can make friends with Theo.'

'It will be a voyage of discovery,' I said.

'Yes, my English friend, and for this trip you will be skipper.'

Which I was, and on that cloudless morning I steered the boat out beyond the harbour walls, while Stelios went and sat with Julia and Sarah up at the bow. Theo, who didn't have a lot to say for himself, stood next to me smoking a cigarette. Every so often he ducked down into the cabin and took a swig of retsina, and after half an hour or so he began to open up. He wanted to know about English girls and if they liked to kiss. Innocent, naïve stuff that a teenager will ask when he doesn't know what is going on with his emotions. What he really wanted to talk about was his girlfriend, Callista, and why he couldn't keep his mind on fishing, which had led to the difficulties with Stelios.

'Do you have an older brother who gives you trouble?' he asked.

Hearing Theo's side of things made me think that maybe Stelios was the one with the problem, resenting his younger brother's freedom.

Meanwhile, Stelios seemed to be thoroughly enjoying himself in the company of the girls, showing no interest in where we were, leaving Theo and me in charge.

Sarah came over and asked if there was anything she could do, saying she felt a bit of a gooseberry.

'Yes, actually. Could you take the tiller while I go and help Theo let out the nets?'

As we ate lunch, Stelios showed off, walking about the boat balancing a bottle of retsina on his head. He was hard on Theo, letting him drink only one glass, while he flirted openly with Julia. Sarah and I just looked at one another. It was obvious what was going on. Theo watched it all silently, overshadowed by his brother.

The schools were now closed until the autumn and the tourist season was in full swing. Many Greek-Americans had come back to their families for the summer months, but it appeared that few foreigners made Ikaria their prime destination. Most were on their way to somewhere else. Like Julia and Sarah, they turned up at odd hours, not just on the ferry from Athens but on much smaller boats coming from other islands. These tended to bring the more adventurous, who would only stay a few days, waiting for another boat, before travelling on.

That was how we met Paulo and Francesca, two Italian punk rockers who walked into the taverna with rucksacks on their backs, arriving from Samos after hitching a ride on the potato boat. They were a strange species I had not come across before. Francesca's hair, dyed the colour of a wheat field, had what looked like a footpath cut through the middle of it. Her purple eye make-up and the safety pin stuck in her nostril turned a few heads in the taverna. Paulo wore black eyeliner, which gave him a ghoulish look similar to Christopher Lee in *Dracula*, while his hair was streaked with red and blue stripes, like those in Aquafresh toothpaste. They both wore tight dark jeans with chains hanging in loops over their buttocks.

Yannis didn't give them a second look, showing them to a table as he would anyone else, and leaving a menu. We asked if they'd like to join us and before they had even sat down Sam said, 'Why have you got a safety pin through your nose?'

Seeming to ignore him, they went round the table introducing themselves. When they reached Sam, who stuck out a hand, Francesca said in a delightfully rich Italian accent, 'We are making a statement.'

Not the kind of response an eight-year-old boy would have understood, or anyone else sitting around the table.

'What is this statement?' Lottie asked.

'It is about personal freedom,' replied Paulo, 'the individual being allowed to express himself.'

I whispered to Gregory, 'I think this could lead to our first political debate.'

He nodded enthusiastically. I was preparing for an evening of intellectual argument, full of alternative views. After all, gathered around the table we had plenty of nationalities: Canadian, Dutch, Italian, Welsh, and me an Englishman. It was a pity Julia and Sarah weren't here, but Maria told me they had gone to Aghios Kirikos for the evening.

We had all started eating when the evening took a dramatic change in direction. Datsun Jim pulled up, with a goat tied to the cement mixer in the back of the pick-up, chewing a mouthful of hay. Not Jim, the goat.

He wasn't alone and I realised the man with him must be Giorgos. I had quite forgotten that he was coming to the taverna; now at last we could sort out the money he owed me. I hoped it wouldn't turn into an argument in front of our visitors.

Datsun Jim pointed me out to him and he came straight over. The rounded belly must have been a family trait, or maybe Giorgos was a man of hamburgers and booze, because his T-shirt bulged, displaying on the front a blonde beauty in a black leather jumpsuit holding a smoking gun. He took no notice of anyone but me, and in a strong Greek-American accent said aggressively that he had no intention of paying me any money.

Before I had a chance to say a word, Ros was on her feet.

'What a bloody cheek! How dare you come in here and refuse to pay my husband for days of work he has done on that house of yours while your brother just drinks endless cans of Coke and then disappears for the day?'

That rather took him by surprise, but as he was about to respond, with mounting anger and clenched fists, Ros got going again.

'I bet you haven't even brought the money. Show it to us. Where is it?'

At this point, Maria came running from the kitchen carrying a broom and whacked him on the arse, simultaneously berating him in a tirade of Greek, letting him know where her loyalties lay.

Paying her scant regard, Giorgos pulled a bundle of drachma from his pocket and threw it down on the table in front of me. Everyone in the taverna had stopped eating, all knives and forks resting on unfinished plates of food.

'Double or quits,' he said, looking straight at me.

'What do you mean?'

'We arm-wrestle. You say I owe you two thousand five hundred, we wrestle for five thousand drachma.'

'Don't be stupid,' said Ros, back on her feet again. 'Pay what you owe, and walk away with your dignity.'

I didn't say anything. I was staring at Giorgos's arms, which looked fat and flabby. Having been a hill farmer, carrying pigs weighing a hundred and forty pounds and clearing stones from acres of fields, I had, despite my thinness, a deceptive strength.

I looked at Ros. I had never seen such seething anger on her face before. Sam and Lysta had their arms around their mother's waist. Seth was preoccupied with his pencil box, which was full of dead insects.

'Here,' said Giorgos, picking up the money. 'I give the five thousand to Jim, and he gives it to the winner . . . you agree? Otherwise I walk out of here, and I give you nothing.'

Ros was silent and then, with a surrendering wave of her hand, said, 'Oh, I don't care any more.' She sounded defeated.

Gregory said to me quietly that he thought Giorgos had been drinking, and although he was large, it didn't necessarily mean he was strong. 'I think you can win,' he said encouragingly.

Lottie couldn't grasp what was going on and asked Ros to explain how all this had come about.

'OK,' I said, taking up Giorgos's challenge. 'I will arm-wrestle you for five thousand drachma.'

I needed a few minutes to prepare, to choose the best table; most of them were wobbly on the uneven ground. And I wanted Gregory to act as my second. It was a sultry evening, unusually still, with not even the gentlest of breezes wafting in from the Aegean. Apart from Francesca and Paulo, everyone was in T-shirts and shorts, their skin damp with sweat. All Datsun Jim said to me was, 'I told you he was angry.'

'I don't think it matters now.' There was no point in saying any more, although there was much I could have said. After all, it was only because of his blundering incompetence that I was facing this situation.

'Good luck, my friend,' he said in a soulful way, with a look of regret in his eyes.

'So you do have a conscience?'

'I do not understand this word.'

We agreed on the table to be used and placed it in the middle of the taverna. Giorgos and I chose our chairs and sat down. I calmed myself by taking several deep breaths, flexing my fingers. The last thing I wanted to do was show the most obvious sign of fear, a trembling hand, which I had done once, leading to my downfall in the school conker championship. All I had to do was get myself into the right frame of mind.

At this point Sam came over to me, I thought to give his father some moral support. 'I don't think you can win, Dad. He's as big as a whale.'

Ros had positioned herself just a few feet away and was perfectly placed to be in my line of vision.

And then, finally, we interlocked our hands and brought our elbows together. If they rose from the table, even slightly, the contest would be halted, and we would begin again. Whoever forced the other's hand on to the table would be declared the winner.

Gregory began the countdown, 'Three . . . two . . . one', and for the first few seconds Giorgos and I just looked at each other, neither of us wanting to give away how much energy we were expending. Both forearms upright, we held a rigid position, until Giorgos gradually increased his effort, forcing my wrist back three or four inches. Gregory, who was close to the action, kept leaning forward saying, 'Hold him, buddy . . . just hold him there.'

Datsun Jim was not encouraging his brother. Instead he stood behind him and opened a can of Coke before sticking a toothpick into an olive.

Then suddenly everything became more dramatic. Perhaps Giorgos was frustrated by my not conceding any further advantage to him, but in a careless split second he let out a groan and threw every ounce of his strength at me. I knew that if I could withstand the full onslaught, he would be a spent force. His face started to go through an ever-changing sequence of grotesque contortions, similar to those you see in a hall of mirrors at a funfair.

Just when I thought he was done, he made a last desperate attempt, his eyes bulging. But he still couldn't force my hand down, and I could tell he was weakening. With one supreme effort, I flattened his arm against the tabletop and it was over. His head flopped on to his forearm.

Gregory leapt forward and raised my hand in the air. I could see mixed emotions on Ros's face, but whatever she was thinking we were better off by five thousand drachma, which Datsun Jim wasted no time in passing to me. Was he really being serious when he whispered in my ear, 'Could you lend me five hundred?'

I nearly burst out laughing.

'Only for a few days . . . then I pay you back.'

I hadn't a single word for him. What would have been the point? He was not the type of man to reflect on the evening's events. Tomorrow he would wake up and begin another day's work on Giorgos's house, be distracted once more and wonder where the morning had gone. If he remembered, he would move his goats to another spot, take a siesta, and curse himself for leaving the shovel to harden in a pile of cement.

'Now, where were we,' said Gregory, 'after that rude interruption? Oh yes, our rousing political debate.'

When the others had gone I had one last Amstel and Maria came and sat with me, her hair coming undone from the tortoiseshell clip she always wore. In all the time we had been here, I'd never seen her eat or have a drink, but tonight she sipped a glass of cloudy lemonade with me.

'You will remember your time here, I think, yes?' she said with an ironic smile. I could have talked to Maria then, now that the place was quiet, but Sarah and Julia appeared, returning from their evening out. They seemed happy, giving one another conspiratorial looks, as if something exciting had happened. But whatever it was they weren't going to tell me tonight.

I went home and when I got into bed, without waking Ros, I put JJ Cale's album *Naturally* into the cassette player and listened to 'Magnolia'. It's one of those tracks that you can float away on in the minutes before sleep, gently slipping into a dream.

9

A Way of Life

Three days before, I had posted a long-overdue letter to my mother. It had been a rambling account of our life on Ikaria, with a certain amount of poetic licence, which my mother adored anyway. And then one of those inexplicable coincidences happened, as when after a long silence someone comes into your thoughts and that same day they get in touch. I picked up an embossed Basildon Bond envelope from the Poste Restante in Aghios Kirikos and recognised her handwriting.

I read my mother's letter on the harbour wall, where I'd come looking for Stelios. It was full of down-to-earth things that had been keeping her awake at night. She reminded me that I was twenty-nine years old, with a growing family who needed a sense of security and an education to prepare them for their life ahead. And what was I doing exactly, living on a Greek island, but enjoying a long holiday? Did I have any idea when we were coming home, and was I intending to get a proper job? I was disappointed to read this, because I had explained how well the children were doing in the letter now on its way to her, and how serious Ros was about teaching them. But it was written, no doubt, after a bad night's sleep, and full of the worry that mothers have about wayward sons. I imagined her pacing up and down her sitting room, picturing all sorts of disasters. I'd have to telephone and try to reassure her that everything was under control, and her grandchildren were thriving.

That's what was going on in my head when Stelios walked past, close enough for me to put my hand on his shoulder and say, '*Kali mera. Ti kanis?*'

And after absorbing my mother's woes I was treated to Stelios's, presented in a way only a Greek could, with all the passion that probably built the Greek Empire. He said his wife was complaining he was no longer a loving husband.

'So I have a weakness for women, you understand? She is jealous if they want to come out on the boat. But I say yes, they should come.'

'You are taking girls out on your boat?'

'Of course. They come as tourists . . . I tell my wife we make money.'

What was I meant to say? What could I do other than listen to his troubles?

'Are we still going fishing together?'

'Of course, later this week. I will telephone you at the taverna.'

I knew Stelios liked to flirt, having seen him that morning with Julia. He was a fisherman out in the Aegean; what was more romantic than that? His way of life would capture the heart of any young girl, especially coming back into Aghios Kirikos under a setting sun. Stelios would no doubt appear a seductive figure and he'd be unable to resist the temptation.

Walking the coast road back to Lefkada, you were never far from a beach where you could pull off your T-shirt, kick off your sandals and run into the cooling sea to float on your back, looking up into a blue sky. I did it often, ambling along in the heat, past the fig trees and the prickly pears, taking a slow walk home in the sun. Then I'd skim stones across the smooth clear surface of the water, thinking about work, feeling uncertain about all sorts of things. Stelios was unpredictable, Datsun Jim now no more than someone I passed on the road.

That's what was occupying me when I saw Sarah and Julia, both in bikinis, down on the beach. I went down to join them and we talked as we swam away from the shore, enjoying the stillness of the morning. Afterwards we sat on the rocks chatting, while Julia combed her hair and then, taking off her bikini top, walked off to look for shells. Sarah and I had fallen into the habit of reminiscing about England and I told her the only things I missed were the month of May, hawthorn blossom and a cottage loaf. 'Actually, there are four things. I miss cricket too.'

Then in one sentence she swept me a long way from England.

'I've met someone,' she said. 'An Ikarian.'

At first I didn't know what to say. 'When?' I asked finally.

'The other evening, when Julia and I went into Aghios Kirikos.'

'Oh, so that's why you were giving each other those looks in the taverna?'

'Probably. It's exciting.'

'Does this mean you might be staying on Ikaria a bit longer?'

'Well, we've no plans to leave.'

⌐

When I eventually got back to Lefkada, Vassili's car was parked below our house, the back seat full of children sitting on one another's laps and Ros insisting they go on without her, telling them she would hitch a ride.

'You're not kidnapping our children again?' I said, it having become a standing joke between us.

'This time we will charge you a ransom,' shouted Vassili, struggling to be heard above the din coming from behind him.

'Mum, Seth's too heavy. Can't Sam have him on his lap?'

Seth pulled up his T-shirt to inspect his stomach. 'I'm not fat, Mum.'

'No, you're not at all,' said Ros, 'but it's probably best you sit on Sam's lap.'

And so it went on, as the adults tried to manoeuvre six children to fit comfortably into a sardine tin. Then, just as they had all quietened down, along came Mercedes – a human being, not a car – in his pick-up selling *karpuzi* (watermelons), blasting out his unintelligible sales pitch through a megaphone. At this time of year it was a daily occurrence: you would hear him some way off, gradually growing louder as he made his way to Lefkada. Maria and Yannis always bought from him, *karpuzi* so large they could only carry one at a time.

So we asked for a lift and sat up front with him, while every hundred yards he bawled out, 'Watermelons, come and get your fresh watermelons.' Or so I guessed. But nobody appeared, probably because everyone was on the beach, or taking a siesta. The lack of customers didn't deter Mercedes, who, if anything, increased the volume.

When we pulled up behind Vassili's car some twenty minutes later, Mercedes threw me a *karpuzi* as heavy as a medicine ball. Ros gave him fifty drachma and left her hand out, expecting some change.

'Why are you doing this with your hand?'

'Does a *karpuzi* cost fifty drachma?'

'No, eighty . . . for you it is cheaper.'

'Why?'

'Because of your children. They look Greek, yes?'

'Tell me about this game called cricket your son wants to play,' said Vassili, who always sunbathed with a pair of shorts on his head.

'It's a very old English game that we have been playing for over two hundred years, but we need a bat and ball.'

'Draw me this bat. I will make one,' he said, searching for a piece of paper.

'We need three stumps as well.'

'What is this unusual word stump? I've never heard it before.'

'I'll draw one for you, then if you can make them we can play cricket.'

'Of course. I have plenty of time.'

It started off a conversation about Vassili's simple philosophy of life. It was what we are all striving for: to make enough money and still have time to do other things.

'To understand an Ikarian you must know his way of life,' Vassili told me. 'Time is easily wasted here, and if everyone is doing it there is little choice but to sit and talk and be sociable. No one is in a hurry; the world will go on changing regardless of what we believe in Ikaria. Many of the houses being built are for those who work in America, in Pittsburgh and Detroit. It is they who bring back their dollars. These houses you see are the slowest houses ever built anywhere in the world. They wait for those who will one day return home and be Ikarians again, and live our way of life. Slowly. *Siga, siga.*'

He was probably right. Life is easier when the cost of living is cheap and you have long hot summers to enjoy. Ikarians kept everything simple; most of what they ate they had grown or caught themselves. Ros and I understood that way of life, the only difference being that I liked to get out of bed with a bit of enthusiasm. That was one thing a lot of Ikarians did not have first thing in the morning, and so the day took a long time to get started. Most Ikarians would not survive for five minutes on a Welsh hill farm, having to be up at six, carrying a bale of hay on your back in darkest winter, searching for sheep.

No one found it necessary to show what they had achieved, because no one competed and no one had great material ambitions in the first place. Vassili and Agathi seemed content, both in their late thirties and not short of money. When I asked Vassili what he did for a living, he told me he had a printing business in Athens. For Agathi, there was nothing to do now but enjoy the long school holidays.

Ros was obviously very happy on Ikaria and it crossed my mind that soon we could be talking about a more permanent life here.

5.

Gregory the Gregarious had taught Sam how to tell the time and lent him his watch, and ever since then Sam had been asking everyone to guess the time. The novelty was wearing a bit thin.

'*Ti ora einai*, Dad?'

'What does that mean?'

'What's the time in Greek. Julia taught it to me.'

'Three minutes later than when you last asked me.'

'Wrong, Dad. Only two minutes later.'

'Well, I always told you time flies.'

That evening we were going to the *panagiri* over in Galiskari, on the north side of the island. It was an all-night festival, and most of us at Lefkada were going. I wondered whether we'd see Julia and Sarah over there. I hadn't seen them for a few days and knew they were keen to go to a *panagiri*.

Paulo and Francesca had found some marijuana growing out in the wild, not far from the Toula Hotel building site. It was a couple of kilometres away, set back off the road to Aghios Kirikos, where building had started in the spring. Marijuana didn't grow in the wild on Ikaria, as far as I knew, so someone must have planted it. They asked us all if we smoked the stuff, and it didn't surprise me that everyone was up for a night getting stoned. They put some joints together, much longer and fatter than the ones we rolled back in Wales.

Galiskari was an hour and a half away, and no one had given a thought to how we were going to get there.

I did, when I saw Datsun Jim stop at the taverna and count out several drachma, obviously settling a debt with Maria. When he saw me he couldn't restrain himself, and I had to endure a hug that reeked of old goat. He delighted in telling me Giorgos had gone to Mykonos to stay with cousins for over a month.

'Now we can work together again.'

'No we can't,' I told him bluntly.

'But I have money, look,' showing me what must have been ten thousand drachma. There was no subtlety to Jim. 'It's from my brother to build the house.'

'Can you get rid of the cement mixer and drive us to Galiskari? We'll pay for your petrol . . . will you do it?'

'Of course, for you, and then we work together again.'

That I didn't answer. I could imagine how Ros would react. Divorce me, probably.

'I come back in half an hour.'

I knew Datsun Jim's half-hours, but didn't react fast enough. He was gone, narrowly missing Mercedes coming the other way, still flogging his *karpuzi*.

It had been some time since I'd been alone with Lottie, and I could tell there was something on her mind when she asked if we could go for a walk. She had been sleeping on the beach for a while now and was running out of money, but Maria had offered her a job waitressing for a hundred drachma a night. Yannis had been demoted to dishwashing after the fiasco that had happened a few nights before when a group of businessmen from Athens had come for supper and not one of them had got what he ordered. Earlier Gregory had seen the men rolling out architectural drawings over the bonnet of a parked car, below the Toula Hotel now under construction. In his opinion, they were big city boys with bags of money and, no doubt, commercial ideas on how to exploit the island.

I didn't think Lottie wanted to go for a walk just to tell me about her job with Maria. Then she said, as if asking for a reference, 'What do you think of Gregory?'

'He's a great guy. One of those people I'll have a long friendship with, I hope, long after we have all left Ikaria,' I replied without hesitation.

'You know that already?'

'Yes, I do. Why, is there a problem?'

'I am sleeping with him, that's all.'

As we walked on Lottie told me how confused she was, feeling guilty about her past lover, even though he had left her with a broken heart. I didn't understand why she should feel disloyal to someone who had hurt her so badly and just said, 'Have a fling with him. What have you got to lose?'

'That's what Ros said.'

'I agree with her. Have some fun.'

ſ.

We all piled into Datsun Jim's pick-up. Lottie and Ros sat up front, the rest of us in the open at the back. As we were leaving, Maria said in her best broken English, 'If you let Jim drink, he will kill you all.'

It was a stark warning, but right on the button. The evening sky was filling with stars, among them the constellations of Orion and the Plough that guided mariners across the ancient Aegean. I knew this because Stelios had pointed them out to me. Dust swirled in ochre clouds and hid the road behind us. The ride was exhilarating as the island darkened into mountainous outlines and the evening around us became burnished with gold in a fading radiance.

Jim showed no consideration for his passengers. We bounced up and down and swerved round corners until we had to thump on his window.

'Slow down! The children are going to be sick!'

After an hour or so everyone needed a break and so we stopped for a while and Paulo lit a joint. We passed it between us, looking at the lights coming from the isolated houses dotted upon the hills. After a bout of giggling we sat silently, listening to the bells of a herd of goats passing in the night. I think we were all entranced; it was a sound that must have been heard since biblical times. We didn't offer Datsun Jim a drag on the joint; luckily for us he was happy with his cans of Coke and Karelias.

By the time we got to Galiskari I was expecting the children to show signs of tiredness, but their adrenalin was flowing as we drove down on to the flat sandy beach with its white waves rolling in, exploding over the rocks. Out on a promontory a small blue and white church shone in the moonlight.

Amongst the milling crowd, plates of food were being carried to a long line of trestle tables. Fish were neatly arranged in circular displays laid out like mosaics within rings of lemon slices. These works of art were carried by women wearing traditional costumes, with brightly coloured woven head scarves. And then even more food appeared: roasted goat, salads, cheeses and bowls of olives. Everyone queued in a long line that stretched across the sand.

Fires were lit on the beach and out came the bouzouki players and violinists, while village children in long skirts shook their tambourines. It was a clear night, and under the vaulted heavens, around bonfires that crackled and threw their embers like fireflies into the air, the music began. A single file of dancers emerged out of the crowd, hands on each other's shoulders, and in amongst them I saw Sarah and Julia. They moved in unison with precise steps, lifting their bended knees, swaying at the hips, turning their faces to and fro, leaving their footprints in the sand. It was poetry in slow motion, and as others started to join them Ros grabbed me, even though I had a plate in one hand and a mouth full of goat.

'You know I can't dance,' I choked.

'Come on. Give your plate to Sam.'

And so, in a completely uncoordinated way and out of step with everybody else, I moved in my own time. Lysta came over to me and summed it up in one sentence. 'You look silly, Dad.' She was right, but Ros didn't care.

Lottie and Gregory could have been Greek dancing for years. It just showed, you either have rhythm or you don't.

Meanwhile, Datsun Jim had found himself a rather large woman, who looked at him lovingly in the firelight, her teeth shining like piano ivories. He was more than a foot taller than her and couldn't reach her waist, so had placed both hands round her neck. It looked as if he was about to strangle her. They shuffled from side to side, moving to a strange beat of their own, reminiscent of the mating dance of exotic birds.

Everybody was having a good time, and the children perked up even more when they saw Vassili and Agathi in the crowd. Christos and Sam immediately disappeared with a football, while Lysta, who showed a natural rhythm, danced with Xenia. Seth amused himself beneath us, looking for little things that had expired in the sand.

'He's a natural born undertaker. Instead of digging up the dead, we've got to teach him to bury them,' I told Ros.

'I hope you're not being serious.'

It was three o'clock when a wave of tiredness came over me. I went looking for Paulo and Francesca, who I found drawing in the sand with long sticks. That's what marijuana can do to you: concentrate the mind, get you deeply absorbed in things.

'What is it?' I asked.

'The end of the world.'

Francesca said it was beautiful because when the tide came in it would be washed away, leaving no trace. 'It symbolises our own lives.'

Now was not the time for a deep discussion. I was trying to gather our group together, and see if everyone was happy to go back to Lefkada.

'We can go when you want,' said Paulo, with a casual shrug of the shoulders.

I found Gregory and Lottie propped up against some natural rock armchairs, staring dreamily into the night sky.

'It's so groovy out there in space,' Gregory said when he saw me, more than a little laid back.

I'd done my bit of star-gazing for the night and said, 'Yes, but out there it takes light years for anything to happen.'

'That's so true, man.'

'Are you ready to head back to Lefkada?'

'Ready when you are.'

All I had to do now was find Datsun Jim, and I went in search of him along the beach. Around me the music played on. People were still dancing, teenagers running in and out of the sea, barking dogs leaping into the waves.

I eventually found him fast asleep on the sand. Lying next to him was his unconscious lady friend, who rather resembled a ship's figurehead, except that her breasts were rising and falling. Through her half-open mouth she emitted a noise as if she were shunting railway carriages. I tried shaking Jim awake, relieved that his breath did not smell of alcohol.

'Jim . . . are you OK to drive us home?'

He didn't say anything at first, and then rolled over and looked at her.

'Thekla,' he said, and began speaking to her in syrupy Greek, but she was dead to the world.

'You help me carry her?' he asked, obviously wanting to bring her with us. And I did for a few feet, but she was heavier than a donkey.

'It's no good, Jim. She can't come with us.'

He looked at her longingly, planted a heavy kiss on her mouth and left her, a large heap in the sand.

'This, you know, is my first ever woman. I love her,' he said, looking back at her. 'I will drive you to Lefkada, and then I return, and bring her home.'

10

Artemis

It seemed Sister Ulita had only one friend. Artemis turned up from Athens at odd times and stayed for a few days before disappearing again. Where to I could only guess, but I didn't think it was back to Piraeus, for no one could have endured the eight-hour voyage so often, nor the cost, although she looked like a woman of means; she always took a taxi back to Aghios Kirikos.

I knew when Sister Ulita was expecting her because she made a fuss about my appearance, making me throw water over my face, indicating that I should tidy myself up, or at least shake the dust off my shirt. When we were on our own and ate together, she didn't seem to mind how I looked. Why did she like me clean and well presented whenever Artemis came to the monastery?

Often, I had lunch with them, and while they talked I got on with eating my meal, usually a Greek salad. Sister Ulita acknowledged me only occasionally, when I would say 'Kala', letting her know how much I was enjoying it. In England, the gardener would have had his lunch alone in a potting shed, drinking tea from an enamel mug.

When we had finished, Artemis was always the first one on her feet, clearing the table of plates and cutlery and returning from the kitchen with a bowl of fresh fruit grown in the monastery garden. She never cleared the place laid for the unexpected guest, who yet again would have failed to arrive.

Sister Ulita insisted on this ritual, believing that even at the final moment the bell could ring and a weary traveller fall across the threshold. Having outrun the pirates who attacked and robbed the Ikarians, he would be in urgent need of sustenance. So the empty seat at the end of the table was of great significance, and no one should ever discount the possibility of a late appearance. The fact that this had not happened for at least two hundred years did nothing to diminish the potency of the ancient custom. At the end of the meal, Sister Ulita would sit in the empty chair, put her hands together and utter a silent prayer. This signified that lunch was over, and no day was any different.

Her serene face gave nothing away, not least because she was never without her sunglasses, and unable to look into her eyes, I was naturally drawn to her mouth. I watched the movement of her lips, sometimes taut, or expanding with a smile, depending on her mood. Although we understood little of each other's language, I learnt how to lighten the expressions on that enigmatic face, and even to make her laugh, by enacting no more than a series of comedy skits: deliberately tripping over a flagstone, or standing on the end of the hoe so that it came up and nearly hit me in the face, a finale I generally managed to prevent, catching it at the last moment. They were scenes I remembered from silent films and I was determined, since coming to work for her, that I wouldn't be some distant figure who just raised his hat at the end of the day and said, in his best Greek, '*Kali spera*' (Good evening) and walked away. With so few words between us, these humorous acts transcended our lack of language.

When she disappeared to take her siesta, I too would drift off on the wooden bench in the shade of a pear tree, listening to the cicadas' incessant screeching, after pulling my ripped panama hat over my face. That hat was a tight fit since I'd once had to retrieve it from the Aegean. I should never have dried it in the sun.

If Artemis had a siesta, it was always a quick one. She would appear in the quiet hours after lunch, having just showered, her hair combed and wet, her eyes dark with mascara; she had the look of an Italian contessa. I'd be woken by the flick of her cigarette lighter, but pretend to still be sleeping until she came and stood over me. I could not ignore the sound of her footsteps on the flagstones. She spoke with a certain aloofness, as if I should be made aware of potential dangers, when she told me that she'd noticed I had fair skin and could burn easily. Something, of course, I had known all my life.

'You have freckles, and already the back of your neck is red,' she said, knowing I could see her brown legs and shoulders glistening with sun cream, her dress so light it fluttered around her knees, while a cloud of smoke from her cigarette floated above her. Artemis was a sophisticated Athenian and our conversations became intriguing little intervals in the long blue afternoons. I'd no idea whether there was any deeper meaning behind them. They never really went anywhere, but she fascinated me and then would be gone, leaving the scent of her perfume lingering in the air.

Who was this woman who had entered the nun's enclosed life? I knew she wasn't the unexpected visitor, for Sister Ulita had always prepared her room by the time the taxi dropped her at the monastery gates. Although the nun led an isolated life she was not completely cut off from the outside world, for there was a telephone in her sleeping quarters. Whenever it rang, she would gather up the loose skirt of her habit and run as if her life depended on it, such was her obedience to this second calling. But if she was at prayer, the chapel door did not open and the telephone was left to ring.

Once, when I was sweeping the flagstones in the shadows of the cypress trees, an intense sound engulfed the courtyard, as the telephone rang and the cicadas screeched in unison, shattering the tranquillity of the monastery. Suddenly, much to my relief, both ceased as if a click of fingers had ordained an instant silence. And a strange feeling came over me as I stared at the whitewashed walls; the shadows darkened and the bright colours of the bougainvillaea by the kitchen door intensified. I felt as if I was a figure in a painting, such was the stillness that surrounded me. Then a breeze from the Aegean stirred the dust, blowing pine needles across a patch of parched earth. A coil of rope became a snake, and slithered away through the rosemary. I knew then that I was hallucinating. I'd had too much sun.

Sister Ulita came to get me for lunch and must have seen something was wrong, because she immediately moved me into the shade and turned the hose on me. She gave me several glasses of water, repeatedly saying, '*Nero, nero,*' slapping the back of my hand like a mother scolding a child.

I felt all right half an hour later, if a little light-headed, and ate a peach. I hadn't realised I was getting dehydrated because it wasn't a feeling I was familiar with. Hardly something one experiences often in North Wales, although the summer of drought in 1976 was a crazy time.

This incident curiously altered the way Sister Ulita behaved towards me. She appeared more relaxed and certain of herself and became more involved in what I was doing, showing me the depth to dig down to in a patch of land, or the exact distance to leave between each row of seedlings to be transplanted. Everything was expressed silently, as if by a mime artist, with a wagging finger, a shaking or nodding of the head, a clapping of hands and 'Bravo' when she was happy.

After her siesta, she would sit with Artemis, the two of them embroidering a large altar cloth spread out along the length of the table where we ate our lunch. Their hands rose and fell with a regular, unchanging rhythm, drawing golden threads through the fabric. Despite her arthritis, Sister Ulita could hold a needle. Their pace never altered, even as they talked. I could see now what these two friends shared, and it became part of everyday life whenever Artemis was here. Just behind them, beside the whitewashed church, a cloud of swallowtail butterflies danced in a flowering buddleia. The scene made me realise that I wouldn't mind at all if time stood still, if only for a little while.

In that long summer of hot afternoons the weather rarely changed, and neither did the routine I followed. After the sun had slipped behind the mountains I made the slow walk up the sloping bank to the sluice gate. Opening it no more than a few inches, I watched the water rush and run along the trenches, quenching the thirst of aubergines, peppers and tomatoes, the smell of the earth filling the air as the water was absorbed into the tilth. Here I would sit and gaze over the monastery roof to the wide expanse of the Aegean, the island of Fourni in the distance, just as it had ever been, in a shimmering haze. It was only the bleating of the goats that got me on the move again. They knew the time of day and I'd walk them to the shelter which was now their milking parlour. That was when Artemis would reappear, a few feet away in the cooling day. I couldn't tell if these visits were premeditated, or whether she'd had enough of sewing and was simply wandering about the place looking for a suitable spot to smoke a quiet cigarette.

She spoke good English, and standing behind me as I milked she told me how grateful Sister Ulita was to have someone she could rely on. There was a soft growl to her voice, I thought with a hint of seduction, but probably what I was hearing was no more than the grittiness that comes from smoking. I never knew what to expect from Artemis, but when she asked me if I was superstitious I stopped milking and turned round to look at her; it seemed an odd thing to ask.

'What do you mean by superstitious?'

'Do you believe certain things have magical powers?'

I answered without really giving it any thought. 'Yes, I do.'

'Tell me one you believe in.'

I wondered where this was heading. 'The imagination' was all I said.

She finished her cigarette. I could hear her stubbing it out under her sandal. 'You can't make me laugh as you do the nun . . . but you can make me smile.'

What was she trying to say? That she knew Sister Ulita and I shared some humorous moments together?

Artemis was finished with me then and walked away through the olive trees in her bright, flowery dress, swirls of dust appearing with every footstep. Maybe I was just a distraction that relieved her boredom. I must have been fifteen years younger than her; she was having fun with me because she could get away with it.

At the end of each day I would sit in the courtyard and Sister Ulita would bring me sweetened orange peel curled around a spoon on a glass dish. And while I ate it and drank a glass of iced water, she put into a wicker basket my wages for the day: yoghurt, cheese, eggs and vegetables. It felt right to be rewarded for my labours by being given food. Not a financial transaction, but a simple act of giving and receiving. If I could have explained it in Greek I would have told her how much it pleased me to be paid in this way.

On the walk back to Lefkada, the sea seemed harrowed up in dark blue waves, tipped with white specks like a flock of seabirds, thousands of them. I had my T-shirt tied around my waist, enjoying the cool breeze on my skin. It came over me how content I felt to be leading a life so satisfying and uncomplicated. And I knew Ros and the children were happy here too.

🔲

Lysta was developing strong opinions, mostly about food. She was telling everyone we met that she was vegetarian. It seemed to strengthen her individuality, but was now becoming rather predictable. That evening, when I ordered a chicken stifado, she turned up her nose and asked to leave the table to go and sit with Francesca and Paulo who, she claimed, were teaching her Italian. She was also getting quite competitive with her twin brother, because Sam had started writing down Italian words in his notebook and had decided to show off by reading them out to her: *grazie, mamma mia, prego, signorina.*

I asked Lottie where Gregory was that evening and she said he was off photographing the sunset. He'd got it into his head that he could make money by selling postcards of Ikarian sunsets, because the choice at the kiosk in Aghios Kirikos was terrible: they were out of focus and artificially coloured. He'd decided here was a chance to promote work of a superior quality. I didn't know Gregory was a man with business ideas.

Sarah and Julia joined us then, back from Aghios Kirikos, and Sam seized the opportunity to remind Sarah she had said she would teach him to swim.

'But you can already swim,' I said.

'Only the doggy paddle. That's what Gregory calls it.'

'Yes, of course,' she said. 'Let's do it tomorrow. Come and knock on our door in the morning.'

When Lysta came back to the table, she told us she could say goodnight in four languages.

'Let's hear them.'

'*Kali nicta, Nos dan, Bonne nuit, Buona notte.*'

And just as I was thinking I should go and reply to my mother's last letter Gregory turned up, camera round his neck, full of energy and enthusiasm that never seemed to diminish, no matter what time of day.

'You know, I'm going to have to develop my own shots. OK,

you can take good photos, but you gotta be able to supply the finished product, something you can be proud of.'

'You could come to North Wales and photograph the mountains,' I said.

'Yeah, man, I'm up for that.'

Lottie came over and kissed the back of Gregory's neck. It was the first time I'd seen any affection between them. Gregory didn't respond, probably not wanting to show publicly that he was fond of her. You wouldn't have guessed they were having a love affair. All that Ros and I knew was what Lottie had told us that day.

When we did all leave the taverna, Ros carrying a sleeping Seth in her arms, I experienced again the contentment I'd felt on the walk back from the monastery that afternoon. I didn't know why it came into my mind, but back at the house I asked Ros if she often thought about her father.

'I do, of course, but not with such sadness. Now it's more just remembering him.'

Ros had been very close to her father and it had been a difficult time for her when he died. But we didn't have the chance to say more, because Lysta, after getting ready for bed, came in and started to read to us.

🔲

It was a particularly hot day. Maria had a wooden thermometer hanging from one of the eucalyptus trees and Gregory told me it was eighty-five degrees, '*poli zesti*', so we were all on the beach together, swimming and sunbathing. Sarah was in the sea teaching Sam the crawl as she had promised. It was because he wanted to race Christos, Vassili's eldest boy.

I was lying on a towel half asleep when Vassili appeared and stood above me holding a tennis ball, throwing down the bat and stumps he'd made.

'They look great, Vassili. OK, let's play cricket.'

I thought better of trying to explain the rules. Nobody, unless it's in your blood, can understand them. Ros volunteered to be wicket keeper, and Sam, seeing what was happening, rushed from the sea, wanting to open the bowling. I placed people in various positions, Gregory at silly mid-off, and to get the game going I went in to bat. I hit the ball all over the place, mostly into the sea, and although Julia nearly caught me, I retired not out, not bothering to keep my score.

Agathi didn't last long, clean bowled by Sam, so we let her stay in again and again out of sympathy. Vassili was a natural, although he possessed no graceful shots, hitting everything for six until I caught him.

After the next over, Ros bowling underarm to Lysta who missed every ball, everyone started to get bored. What is it about cricket, I thought to myself, that simply doesn't interest people unless they've played it at school?

'I don't want to play any more,' said Lysta.

'I've had enough as well,' said Ros, going back to sunbathe.

'Me too,' said Agathi.

'I'm going swimming,' said Sam.

Vassili and Gregory decided to head up to the taverna for an Amstel and I was about to join them when Ros called me over and asked me to rub some lotion on to her back. It was a strange concoction that smelt like vinaigrette.

'What on earth is it?' I asked.

'I made it myself. Olive oil, lemon juice and a secret ingredient. We're hoping it will deepen our suntans; we don't seem to be able to get any browner.'

They were all going to try it, Sarah, Julia and Lottie.

'Are you sure it's safe?'

'Of course, and it's a lot cheaper than Ambre Solaire.'

'Well, watch where you put it. Lemon juice can sting.'

11

The Invasion

It wasn't often on a summer's morning I could sit on the patio with a cup of coffee while everyone slept quietly in the house. Gazing through the branches of the eucalyptus trees to a shimmering sea, I thought there was nowhere I'd rather be.

That was until the Ikarian army arrived. Soldiers spilled out of the back of two canvas-roofed lorries, all holding rifles, and lined up on the road outside the taverna. What on earth was going on? Were we about to be invaded by the Turks? Was this it, was this the day? I ran into the house and woke Ros and the children.

'Quickly, get dressed all of you!' I should have included myself, since I was wearing only a pair of boxer shorts. I could hear orders being shouted, getting ever closer.

'Wake up! Get your clothes on! We're being overrun by the army!'

Four soldiers marched up the steps on to the patio. It was frightening, and why were they here – coming to arrest us? The officer gave an impeccable salute and introduced himself as Captain Karalis. He was dressed immaculately in combat fatigues, the uniformed men with him of similar appearance and cleanliness.

Before he said any more, I told him we were English, and my Greek was limited. Ros and the children had gathered around me, and we all waited nervously to hear what Captain Karalis had in store for us. It went through my mind that maybe we were going to be deported. Did we need a visa, having been here so long?

'We must ask you, if you please, to vacate the area for the next four hours . . . take what you need and lock up your house.'

'Can I ask why?' I said, hoping I wasn't overstepping the mark. He did not give a direct answer.

'All the houses of Lefkada must be secured, and please leave the area, no further questions.' He checked his watch. 'You have half an hour . . . I will return.'

Then he went down to the beach, barking orders, turfing everyone out of their tents, telling them to hurry up. I could imagine the soldiers' reactions when they saw a girl emerge with a safety pin through her nose, but maybe Francesca slipped it out before she went to sleep.

On the blast of a bugle, a troop of soldiers ran into the taverna, shuffling their feet, getting themselves into a perfect straight line. Julia and Sarah came out, sleepy but alarmed and as mystified as the rest of us. Then Maria appeared, angrily waving her broom as she was ushered from her house, while Yannis stood on the steps in an antique nightgown, half man, half ghost.

All of us from the houses dotted around Lefkada and the tents on the beach were herded together. Our names were taken and we were led away towards Aghios Kirikos; behind us they barricaded the road. We were like refugees driven from our homes, Maria still with a broom in her hand. She and Yannis had no more idea what the army was up to than the rest of us. After we'd walked just a few a hundred yards we heard a siren wailing, like the warning given before a controlled explosion takes place.

'Maybe they've found an unexploded bomb,' I said to Gregory.

We walked on and came to the fenced-off site where the Toula Hotel was being built. Yannis and Maria shook their fists at this blot on the landscape, watching the bulldozers at work, the ready-mix lorries tipping out their concrete. Maria had never left the island and had always lived a simple life, her father a charcoal burner in the woods around Perdiki. She was probably thinking she was witnessing the ruination of the island in the name of progress, as it's called. We all stood and watched through the wire mesh as they felled trees and dug up the earth.

'Vandals,' said Paulo. 'Destruction of the land for profit.'

Suddenly a black BMW appeared behind us, repeatedly sounding its horn. It was being driven by a dark-suited businessman wearing expensive sunglasses.

'Any of you want work? Good money, bonuses, not Ikarian money.'

It couldn't have come at a better time.

'What kind of money?' I asked.

'Athens money, which means you will get paid. You want a job?' he asked me.

'Yes, maybe. I can mix cement.'

'Go to the office, talk to them.'

'Who are you?' I asked.

'Petros. I am head of the consortium.'

The advancement of tourism had arrived on an island of communists and fishermen, of peasant farmers and café philosophers. Changes were coming; who knew what effect they would have on the people of Ikaria, an island that wanted to be left behind.

But these musings ceased instantly as a volley of gunshots whined through the air. We could hear the repetitive cracking of machine-gun fire. The battle of Lefkada had begun; a little spot on the earth that wasn't even on a map being stormed by the brutish military, with, no doubt, all the wildlife scampering for cover.

We retreated to the beach and had an improvised breakfast: yoghurt, feta cheese and some fruit, all from the monastery, but no one really had an appetite. It all seemed completely unreal, as if a revolution had begun, listening to the distant gunfire while waves broke gently on the shore. We swam and we talked, all wondering what was going to happen to us.

After a while, Sam and Lysta were looking for things to do, Lysta having had enough of practising her cartwheels. Sam was upset that he'd forgotten to bring his snorkel, which I'd bought for him after he'd finally mastered the crawl. But Seth wandered along the beach completely occupied, turning over stones, carrying a wooden coffin under his arm that had once been his pencil box. I watched him, thinking how very satisfying it must be for a small soul to be so absorbed in what he was doing. I hoped this was just a passing phase and couldn't understand the pleasure that he got from little dead insects. He seemed to have no other interests. The day before he had asked Ros to cut one up for him, wanting to see if it had blood. He was only three.

At last one of the soldiers came down and told us we were allowed back and we wandered up to the barricade that was being moved to the side of the road. At the taverna, Captain Karalis sat at one of the tables rolling up maps, and as soon as we approached he saluted us with a beaming smile. It was hard to tell if it was genuine; there was no apology from him for disrupting our morning. He openly admitted that it had been nothing but army manoeuvres, which happened every year somewhere on Ikaria. Even he had not been told until the night before where it would take place. So that was what they had been up to when they took over our homes and closed down the taverna: playing at being soldiers. Around us the troops were clearing up, removing rolls of barbed wire and dismantling their machine guns.

Yannis and Maria completely ignored everything that was going on around them as they opened the taverna and straightened tables. Maria even swept her brush over Captain

Karalis's polished boots, a deliberate act of defiance, waving him aside with an indignant look.

Finally a dozen soldiers got on to their hands and knees. I couldn't imagine what they were doing until I realised they were searching for spent cartridge casings. It was hard to believe they could hold out for long in the event of an invasion if they had to spend half their time retrieving bullets they had just fired.

That evening I knew Sam had been up to something. He looked sheepish and seemed preoccupied. This change in behaviour became more apparent as we sat down for supper on the patio, secretive looks being passed between him and Lysta. I knew that whatever they had been up to, they wouldn't be able to keep it to themselves for long. In the event, they revealed their secret without too much probing. They asked me what my judgement would be of a fictitious person who kept something they had found that didn't belong to them.

'Ah,' I said, 'honesty. We all have to decide about that.'

'Yes, Dad,' said Sam, turning to his twin sister, who nodded in agreement, 'and if this thing that they've found has been lost and the person who lost it will never know, and doesn't need it any more, can they keep it?'

'So it's not worth a lot of money?'

'No, I don't think so, maybe twenty drachma.'

'And it's not useful to anyone?'

'No. It would have been once, but not now.'

'Has it got anything to do with the Ikarian army?' I asked.

'Yes,' he said, unhesitatingly.

'I think I know what it is.'

'How do you know?'

'Has the person who found it got more than one of them?'

'Yes, I think he has.'

'He has, Dad,' said Lysta. 'He's got five of them.'

'Well, if I leave the table and come back in a minute we can decide what to do.'

I walked into the kitchen and poured myself a retsina, and when I returned there on the table lay five brass cartridge casings. Sam and Lysta were looking at me with both hope and guilt on their faces.

'Ah ha,' I said. 'What have we here? Property of the Ikarian army?'

'Yes, but how did you know?'

'I have the mind of a detective.'

Sam and Lysta had found them hunting in the rough scrub at the back of the house, down on all fours for the afternoon. Ros had been surprised they hadn't wanted to go for a swim; now we knew why.

'Can we keep them for ever? I want to take them home with us,' begged Sam.

'You can keep them, but don't let Captain Karalis know. We'll be taken away and questioned for having property that belongs to the Greek army.'

🔲

Datsun Jim could never pull up slowly outside the taverna. He had to slam on everything, causing a great cloud of dust to sweep over the customers eating a quiet meal. It always annoyed Maria, who came at him with her broom raised and began thrashing him in front of everyone. People had to put napkins over their faces, coughing and choking until the dust slowly cleared.

This time, he arrived with Thekla, the love of his life. In extricating her from the front seat, he showed a new side to himself, a touching affection. Manoeuvring her in the limited space the open door provided required not only strength but dexterity. Her white dress, covered with large black circles, made her look like an overweight Dalmatian. Her head scarf was wrapped tightly like a turban. I couldn't see what she had on her feet, probably flip-flops, because she shuffled rather than walked. Watching the two of them, it was hard to imagine what attracted them to each other. When Jim saw me, he did what he always did: came straight over and asked the same question.

'When are we working together again?'

Ros was with me, and it was best for her sake that I showed no interest, which for the first time upset him and he looked crestfallen. I had never seen Ros so angry as that night when I arm-wrestled with Giorgos, and she rightly blamed Datsun Jim for everything.

Jim didn't force the issue; neither did he produce a wad of notes from his pocket. He just stood there and obviously had something on his mind. Then, all in a rush, he said, 'I'm going to marry Thekla, my beautiful woman, and you are to come . . . and you, missus,' he added turning to Ros, who he had never called by her first name, always referring to her as the wife, or your woman, and now missus. Ros and I were a bit taken aback; they had only known one another for a few weeks.

'Well, that is the most wonderful news, Jim,' we both said, almost in unison.

'Now will you come and work for me?' he asked, as if the wedding invitation would somehow tempt me back.

'What about Giorgos?' asked Ros.

'He is leaving in two weeks for Detroit.'

'I don't know, Jim. It is too difficult for me. I need to be paid every day, not as before,' I said.

But Ros, somewhat surprisingly, came up with an idea. What if he was to pay me in advance when he picked me up? That would solve all our problems.

'Yes, this is a good idea. We can shake on it.'

'Do you really want me to do it, go back to work for him?' I asked Ros.

'Why not? You have nothing to lose now.'

'Four hundred drachma,' I said, 'for a morning's work, Jim, then siesta.'

'Four hundred, my friend.'

And so began my new arrangement with Datsun Jim. The next day, arriving nearly an hour late, he got out of his pick-up and before he had even said '*Kali mera*' thrust four hundred drachma into my hand.

'For you, my friend, and now we go to Giorgos's house and you mix the cement a happy man.'

I didn't mention how late he was. Maybe Maria did, waving her arms around and slapping her own forehead in exasperation.

It lasted three days and then the pick-up overheated, so he turned up on a donkey, expecting me to ride with him. But it would have been too much for the poor creature.

'Forget about it, Jim. Let's wait until you get the pick-up fixed.'

'Some fool didn't put water in the radiator.'

'I wonder who that could have been?'

'Why do you look at me like this?'

5

Artemis would often sit reading a paperback, legs crossed on the bench beneath the pear tree. She sat in an upright position holding the book in her right hand, a cigarette in the left. So still was the air the smoke curled upwards and dissipated into nothingness. I was never sure if this elegant posture was a natural pose, for I always sensed she knew I was nearby. And

I couldn't tell whether the book she held in front of her, and seemed so engrossed in, was no more than a prop to tempt me into a conversation. These weren't scholarly books, but well-thumbed Greek love stories, probably bought in second-hand shops, the covers showing lovers in passionate embraces. Maybe after reading them she left them behind for Sister Ulita.

The monastery garden was full of secluded places; Artemis knew them all, and I'd come across her during siesta time, alone, reading these romantic stories. She was an enigmatic woman, who, in her Athenian world, would surely not have been without her male admirers. But here she lived a very different life. It seemed out of character for such a woman to indulge herself with these cheap books and it made me want to discover, even more, what lay beneath the surface.

Her sunglasses rested in her hair and a turquoise dragonfly hovered beside her, as if intoxicated by her perfume. She turned each page with varnished fingernails, smoothing it down as if caressing it. All her movements were graceful, none more so than when she was sewing with Sister Ulita.

Much as I'd wanted to, I'd never asked her why she read these love stories. I thought she might slam the book shut and storm off, offended by my prying. But when a lizard scurried beneath her foot and broke her concentration, I suddenly found myself saying, 'What are you reading?'

'A hopeless love affair. That is all I ever read, love with an unhappy ending,' she said, lowering the book on to her lap and crossing her legs again. I could see by her expression that she was waiting for me to continue the conversation.

'You only ever stay a few days, and then —'

She didn't let me finish.

'It is enough. And besides, I have other things to do. Monasteries, they are like prisons. What do they do but sit in silence and pray.'

'But your work is for the church?' I asked, wondering how long I could engage her.

'I spend most of my time restoring vestments for the bishops on many of the islands. It is tedious work and I'd prefer to be in Athens.'

Then she stretched, with both arms outspread, as one does after sitting for some time, lost in another world. Rather than continue the conversation, she rose and said, 'It is time for some water and fruit,' and walked away, leaving her book behind on the bench, brushing her hair back over her shoulders.

Not long after, I heard Sister Ulita's shrill call, 'Neeko, Neeko.' She never called me once, always twice, as if there was some urgency to it. Which there never had been, and it was the same today, as she appeared with slices of *karpuzi* and a glass of water on a tray, being followed by Perseus, the monastery cat.

As we sat down together she pushed aside the book Artemis had been reading without giving it a second look. She was more interested in attempting to have one of our bilingual chats. She got out her phrase book, and after several pained expressions and false beginnings produced the clearest English I had ever heard her speak.

'Are you enjoying the watermelon?'

To show my delight I applauded her. 'Bravo, bravo, Sister.'

Then I began the laborious task of searching for the correct response, which took nearly five minutes.

'*Ne, efkharisto, karpuzi einai poli auraya.*' Yes, thank you, the watermelon is very nice.

It made me think about the development of language in the first place, of two people sitting in a cave thousands of years ago, wanting to have a natter. The slow progress before that first sentence was spoken, with no phrase book to consult.

She was about to continue when the telephone began to ring and she was off in a rush. Never once had I seen her walk to answer it, just a frantic dash, dropping whatever she was doing.

Artemis, having showered and changed, reappeared wearing a long white dress, as if she was about to attend some important function. There were none on Ikaria that would have required such an extravagant style. It was in keeping with a chic Martini advert, and it showed yet another of the enigmatic quirks of this unfathomable woman.

'You are making good friends with the sister.'

'Yes, I think I am, and soon I hope we will be able to understand each other.'

Whenever I worked at the monastery, the slow-moving afternoons reached an inevitable climax when I walked up the steep incline of the vegetable garden to open the sluice gate. Sometimes Sister Ulita liked to accompany me and watch the water rushing along the trenches, racing between the rows, reviving the plants, leaving the earth damp and the leaves uplifted. But today, as we made our way through the garden, the sky darkened and a light rain began to fall, not bouncing on the leaves, but delicately, as if the heat was dissolving the drops before they reached the ground. It barely ran down my face, just dampened my cheeks, not enough to water the plants or get into the earth. But it stirred the insects who danced in great circles around us. As I opened the sluice gate to release the water, the rain hardened and from nowhere the wind blew up.

Soon I was soaked, my shirt clinging to my body. Because the soil was so dry and dusty the trenches collapsed, and everywhere soon became saturated. All the while, Sister Ulita, who had not run for cover, stood there unmoving in her sunglasses. It was the first time I had been with her in the rain and I could see she was delighting in every drop, because so little fell in the summer months. But she was getting drenched so I said to her, 'Sister, *ela*.' Come.

'*Fidi!*' she replied, as if frozen to the spot.

I didn't know the word – it sounded like 'feethy' – but as soon as I looked down I knew what it meant as I saw a black snake, about six inches long, just two feet from her. It slowly slithered away, eventually disappearing through the dwarf bean plants and she gave a great sigh of relief. '*Thilitiriothis!*' she said. It was poisonous, and a bite could be fatal.

The sudden downpour only lasted a few minutes; the clouds cleared and the intense smell of vegetation filled the air, raindrops dripping from the leaves.

I left Sister Ulita and Artemis sitting sewing the altar cloth, the sun shining again in a clear sky. The nun's last words to me now were always 'God bless you'; Artemis never said goodbye, or acknowledged I was leaving.

12

A Night in the Taverna

Vassili had let me know of a job in Xylosirtis. It was a week's work, painting an upturned fishing boat for the owner of the mini-market, Kostas. His wife was an enormous woman who always wore a black swimming costume, no matter what the time of day or whether she was on the beach or in the shop, which, by the way, never opened or closed. You rang the bell at any time, and if they were there they would serve you. They sold local produce such as fruit and vegetables, milk and cheese. Everything else came from Athens, which explained the half-empty shelves; they were always expecting a delivery '*avrio*'.

Patrolling the front of the shop was a long-haired mongrel with very short legs who emitted a high-pitched yap similar to the sound a toy animal makes when it's turned upside down, only ten times louder. He was on a long lead, and although he had a kennel he preferred to guard his territory by running continuously along a wall that bordered a run of gobbling turkeys, seeing them as a major threat. So whenever I arrived he ignored me, giving his full attention to the bunch of ruffian birds gathered at the wire fence, my approach having set them off.

Like his wife, Kostas also spent all day in his swimming trunks. He was a neat and well-groomed man in his fifties with carefully trimmed hair, grey and wavy, but well maintained. He was muscular, and clearly looked after his sunburnt body. There were striking similarities to the silver-haired man I'd often see on the beach who wanted to attract everyone's attention. Kostas was less flashy, but suave, with a good centre of gravity. He spoke English fluently enough for me not to have to hang on every word, trying to unscramble the meaning of each sentence.

For nearly a week, I left Lefkada at six in the morning to walk the five or so kilometres to Xylosirtis along the quiet winding road, the view of the Aegean coming and going round each bend.

I'd noticed how many Ikarians talked about the wind. Depending on where you lived on the island it seemed to be part of everyday conversation, but at Lefkada it hardly bothered us. How different in Xylosirtis. The Meltemi, as it was called, was tiresome, blowing solidly for five days without a minute's let-up, battering the pines, shaking their branches, bending them in all directions. It was strong enough to blow the cicadas from the trees. That's what Kostas told me, although I didn't know whether it was true. I asked him how he coped and he said if he was in the shop he played loud music, but outside you just had to put up with it. Which I did, starting work at seven, being constantly buffeted on the shore. A few fishing boats moored nearby rocked to the frenzied rhythm of the waves. Sea birds struggling with the Meltemi were seemingly going nowhere, flying on the spot.

There was no one about, apart from Anatoli, an old man I would find every morning sitting on a lobster pot smoking. I hadn't painted a boat before, but Kostas had given me several tins of various colours. It appeared to be a simple job, because all I had to do was repaint what was already there and then put on three layers of varnish. The boat was about fifteen feet long, and rather than having to price it up he paid me four hundred drachma to work until one o'clock each day. It seemed to be the going rate.

Anatoli only moved once an hour, to hobble to the shore and pee into the water. He was at that stage in life when a man has to take into consideration his distance from a public convenience. In Anatoli's case it was fifty yards or so, then take aim into the Aegean. He had an annoying habit of coming over to scrutinise my work when it had absolutely nothing to do with him. He spoke his own version of English, a kind of verbal leapfrog which jumped over words. I managed to understand the gist of what he was saying, but I was trying to concentrate on the job and his interference slowed me down. When Kostas came on Wednesday to see what progress I'd made he tut-tutted, walking around the boat and talking to Anatoli. I could guess what they were saying.

'Bit faster,' was all he said to me, and sauntered off, like a middle-aged Greek god in flip-flops.

When Anatoli eventually left, shortly before one o'clock, I decided to stay on an extra hour and try to make up for lost time. But the wind increased a few knots, blowing dust along the pebbly shore, the grit stinging the bare skin of my back. I gave up and walked to the mini-market to tell Kostas I'd work an extra hour tomorrow and that if Anatoli left me alone I'd get the job done much more quickly. All the way to the shop I battled against the wind, meeting it head on. It turned the feral cats sideways and blew plastic bags down the road. When I got there and rang the bell he didn't answer. I could see him through the window fast asleep on a sofa. Not even the yapping of the mad mongrel dog leaping in the air disturbed him, the turkeys gobbling, their feathers ruffled by the Meltemi.

I was looking forward to getting back to Lefkada, to be somewhere calmer where I could hear myself think; this incessant wind could drive a man insane.

As I got closer to home, the wind dropped and I stopped at a secluded cove, empty but for two people sitting at the far end of the beach.

Wearing only shorts, I kicked off my sandals and walked straight into the sea. And then, after no more than a few steps,

I walked straight back out. A shoal of jelly fish, white and ghostly, sinister-looking things, like strange fungi, were coming towards the shore. I'd heard they had an excruciatingly painful sting; apparently, the simplest antidote was to get someone to pee on it, not that I'd ever witnessed this.

Then, some distance ahead of me, I saw the couple walking towards the sea.

I shouted, 'Jellyfish!' and ran towards them, shouting again, 'Jellyfish!'

It was only then that I recognised Sarah.

'Nick! What are you doing here?' she said, obviously surprised to see me somewhere other than Lefkada and while she was with her Greek boyfriend, who had clearly won her heart. I could see it in her eyes. I knew he was an Ikarian, and now I could see he was slim with a mass of dark curly hair, roughly my age.

'This is Ilias,' she said, and he shook my hand and then took from his pocket a silver tin of tobacco.

'You roll your own,' I said.

'Yes, Golden Virginia. I don't smoke very much, but I buy it whenever I'm in Athens.'

'I haven't had a roll-up since I've been here.'

'Please, help yourself.'

And I did, and smoked one with him as he told me a bit about himself. The islanders called him the Pharaoh; both his parents were Ikarian but he'd grown up in Egypt where his father had been a cotton merchant in Alexandria. Ilias had travelled all over the place and had worked in London and the US.

'By the way, you know what the Ikarians say about these jellyfish?' he said.

'What?'

'That the Turks send them over to frighten the tourists away. Sarah tells me you spend a lot of time at the taverna. I inherited it from my father. I've rented it to Maria and Yannis for years now.'

'It's our second home. We're there every night.'

'You like Maria's cooking?'

'More than that. It's the centre of our universe.'

In the taverna that evening, Paulo and Francesca, who were planning to leave at the weekend, demanded that we debate anarchy and how it could bring about a new way of life, rather than living under the thumb of the political elite.

'Sounds like a subject to get our teeth into,' I said enthusiastically. Not that I knew the first thing about anarchy, only that it was a form of chaos.

'It's a very serious subject,' said Gregory. 'I suggest it should be discussed without too much alcohol being consumed.'

Of course he didn't mean a word of it, and after what had begun as a civilised discussion, voices became raised and gradually we were talking over each other and then shouting. That's when Maria came over waving her broom and said, 'No more drink.'

Nobody had won the argument, and nobody had changed their mind about what they believed. Lottie wanted cars to be banned from all cities in favour of bicycles; Ros and I couldn't think of anything better than democracy. Paulo and Francesca were outnumbered, and, I thought, talking a load of political bollocks; I hadn't been able to resist pointing out the irony of their argument, considering that they came from Italy where governments fell regularly anyway, regardless of whether anarchy was involved.

'If there was anarchy, would we still have to go to school?' Sam asked.

'No, probably not,' I said. 'Everything would come to a halt, and there would be no education as we know it.'

'I want to be an anarchist, Dad.'

'Anyone fancy having a chat about synchronised flower arranging?' I said, trying to lighten up what remained of the evening.

🔣

Just when I thought the night was over, Datsun Jim pulled up with his bride-to-be, Thekla. It looked as if she might have started a diet and Jim's pot belly appeared to have lost a couple of inches as well. They made a constant fuss of each other, Jim offering her his arm as they walked to a table, pushing the seat under her large bottom as she sat down. It was endearing to watch his good manners and the attention he gave her. Unfortunately, he let himself down by clicking his fingers as if he expected Maria to rush over and serve them. Datsun Jim had poured himself into love, and after Maria had brought them a carafe of Ikarian wine they raised their glasses and toasted each other, while from the back of the pick-up a tethered goat bleated its approval.

Jim was the kind of man who would allow himself to be completely dominated by Thekla, which was just as well, as he was incapable of looking after himself. One day, when I had been mixing cement with him, he'd told me that the hardest day of his life had been when he was thirty-six and his mother pushed him out of the family home, having had enough. He'd gone and lived in a goat shed, while the goat went on living there too. He said they had a very good relationship, but I doubted either of them did the washing up.

I knew very little about Thekla, only that she was an Ikarian from Faros, right at the northernmost tip of the island.

While she sipped her soup he excused himself and came over to me.

'She is such a lovely woman,' he said, looking across at her adoringly.

'Jim, you are a changed man. You seem more relaxed.'

'I am very much in love, you can see that. I have given up the Coke. I am on the green beans and the salads. We swim, we walk, life is full of the magic.'

'This is wonderful for you, Jim, after all the years of being on your own.'

'My only worry is the money, the cost of the wedding, very expensive. I have been offered a job, to lay bricks at the Toula Hotel. It is good money, from Athens. Will you come and mix cement for me?'

I hadn't followed up my conversation with Petros on the day of the invasion, but I wondered whether now was the time to do so, so I said, 'I'm painting a boat at Xylosirtis and working at the monastery, but if they will pay me an hourly rate, maybe I could come for four or five hours.'

'This he will do; he needs more workers. You come tomorrow?'

'As soon as I have finished at the monastery.'

🔄

Of all our children, Seth was the most hidden. Trying to fathom what was going on between his ears was beyond us most of the time. When we sat around the table, eating and chatting, he contributed little to the conversation. It was because he had other things on his mind, especially since his discovery of what I thought was a new indestructible compound. Often the world's greatest inventions happen by accident. Two chemicals are brought together by chance, a certain reaction occurs, and quite unexpectedly a new product finds its way on to the market, making someone a millionaire. And it could have been Seth, after he brought back from the taverna the vanilla paste from the bottom of his glass of water. He had crushed the bone-dry bodies of some dead insects into an extremely fine powder which he stirred into the vanilla paste, and left the mixture to dry in the sun, or rather got bored and walked off.

But the sticky substance became rock hard and was impossible to shatter. We hurled it against walls and dropped large boulders on it. We even got a hammer from Maria and tried to smash it. It was simply unbreakable.

'God, Ros,' I said. 'That boy of ours could be an accidental genius.'

'It would be amazing, wouldn't it, but I don't think we should build our hopes up too high,' said Ros. 'It's a long way from here to the shelves of an ironmonger's.'

'You know, Ros, we could have children with hidden talents. We've already produced a fervent vegetarian, an anarchist, and now an inventor.'

She wasn't impressed, reminding me that after the initial excitement had died away something else would come along and distract me. I wanted to do some more experiments, but Maria, who bought the vanilla paste in tubs, became a bit suspicious when I asked her to sell me a kilo of the stuff. She'd already been mystified by watching me trying to smash a little round ball to smithereens with her hammer.

Like everyone else that day, she was a bit on edge since a single-manned submarine had been spotted out in the Aegean heading back to Turkey. Ikaria was rife with rumours of an impending invasion, convinced that this submarine had been on a reconnaissance mission, looking for a suitable place to land troops. The response was to keep a close look-out and soldiers scanned the waters with binoculars, waiting for the Turkish fleet to appear.

Only the older Ikarians considered the threat to be real, remembering their grandfathers' tales, claiming the cursed Turks wanted the island returned to them. It had been in Turkish hands until 1912, when it declared its independence and after five months became part of the kingdom of Greece, so the suspicion was not unreasonable.

Captain Karalis came to the taverna, bringing out the worst in Maria who still hadn't forgiven him. Yannis was more accommodating and treated him like any other customer, including keeping him waiting for his meal. Captain Karalis's assessment, as Ikaria's only professional soldier, was that these threats came in cycles.

'The Turks do it just to let us know they are still out there and to keep us on our toes,' he said, sipping his coffee. 'And I will tell you more. A one-man submarine moving on the surface at five knots surely has a mechanical problem. They need to get it into a garage, and check it over.'

'Of course, captain, you are right. We can breathe again.'

'You do not take me seriously, my friend. One day they will come and try to take our island.'

〈

I knew Datsun Jim would be waiting for me, but it had been an unusual morning at the monastery. One of the goats had a severely injured horn; it had split along its length, right down to the base. Sister Ulita was very concerned, but surprisingly 'hacksaw' was not in the phrase book, and that was what I needed if I was to cut it off. I'd done it before, to cows back on the farm. It causes them no distress and usually they stand quietly, not feeling a thing. Through an improvised mime show and then a sketch, she knew exactly what I was after. She sprang into action with a speed I'd not seen before except when the phone had rung. She kick-started her moped and revved it up on the throttle, and as soon as I opened the monastery gates she raced past me, the loose folds of her wimple flowing behind her. Crouched forward over the handlebars, she leaned into the first corner, her habit ballooning out like a large Christmas pudding. I wished I could have taken a photo. It was the kind of image a rock band would have on the cover of an LP. I walked down a few yards and watched her speeding along the coast road towards Xylosirtis, dust clouds trailing behind her. It was a sight I knew would never fade from my memory.

Half an hour later she returned with a hacksaw, and I cut off the goat's horn.

Datsun Jim was pacing up and down. Now he knew what it was like having to wait for someone. He appeared particularly agitated, sitting on a pile of bricks, chewing his fingernails, no doubt wondering where I was.

'You look worried, Jim. What's the matter?'

'I have given up smoking . . . I don't know what to do with my fingers.'

'God, Jim, you're giving up everything.'

'It's because I love her . . . I do anything for her.'

'What is she giving up for you?' I asked.

'Two loaves of bread a day.'

That I couldn't believe. Jim was prone to exaggeration, but I wasn't going to find out any more just then because Petros appeared, walking around the site with his entourage. Jim said I should ask for eighty drachma an hour, which was the rate the labourers were being paid. If I could choose my hours, I'd be happy with that. It would fit in well with my work at the monastery, and if Stelios ever went fishing again I'd be able to join him. It had been some time since I'd seen him; he hadn't telephoned the taverna for over a week. When I was next in Aghios Kirikos, I'd find out what he was doing.

Petros said he remembered my face when we shook hands. He had a double chin, which would have been a lot more prominent if he'd had his collar done up and been wearing a tie. He was about fifty, going grey, with a receding hairline, accentuated by a high forehead with four lines that came and went depending on his expression. When he was serious he was deeply grooved. He didn't want to talk to me about an hourly rate, telling me to go and discuss it with the site manager. He could have been more courteous. Pushing me into the site office, Jim told me he was like that with everyone, but his money was good and we should work together.

The manager, Zenas, a small man with a lot of hair that seemed to be growing upwards, was pleased to tell me he was no Ikarian but from the Peloponnese, where people were honest and hospitable. He had nothing else to say except that I could have an hourly rate of eighty drachma. He showed me where to clock in and out, and that was it.

Datsun Jim was so pleased that he grabbed me and I had to endure one of his hugs. Expecting the usual stink of old goat, I tried to resist, but no, this time what reached my nostrils was the pleasant aroma of a light perfume that Thekla must have dabbed round his neck. I still didn't enjoy it, but at least it was bearable. Then I walked off site, and Jim said, 'Hey, we work today?'

'*Avrio*,' I said. 'I have things to do in Aghios Kirikos.' As I said it I suddenly realised how naturally Ikarian I was becoming. It used to be me sitting waiting for Jim and getting fed up, but now it was me walking off, telling him *avrio*. I hadn't contrived it; it had just happened.

13

The Birthday Party

I hadn't told Stelios and decided I wasn't going to. It was well past midnight; I always lost track of time out on the Aegean. Only when a dim light slowly brightened on the horizon did I know morning was on its way. It was my thirtieth birthday, and as we headed back to Aghios Kirikos under the fading stars I dwelt on my age and my life so far, while Stelios smoked a quiet cigarette.

My reflecctions upon the significance of turning thirty lasted about a minute. Two dolphins appeared just a few yards from us, the arc of their dive glistening as the rising sun came into view, molten orange, quivering red in a shimmering haze. What a birthday present; even Stelios was on his feet. 'They are beautiful, yes?'

It stirred me to watch them disappearing then reappearing, hardly disturbing the smoothness of the sea, moving as if synchronised, the light spreading over a surface of blue glass. Then, when we thought they were gone, they resurfaced in a watery curve just ahead of the boat, as if they wanted us to follow them.

'I could watch dolphins all day,' I told him.

It had been a good night's fishing. A warm gentle breeze had blown through the nocturnal hours, just as Stelios had said it would; we'd been in our T-shirts all night.

While the nets were down, Stelios tried to teach me to play *tavli*, but I didn't take to it. I preferred to talk, or just absorb the atmosphere of the Aegean rather than roll dice. He said he'd noticed it in me before, that I was lost in the dream of Ikaria.

'What does that mean?'

He didn't answer, not until he'd leant over and opened a bottle of retsina. Then he said, 'I see it in many. You are not the only one.'

'I don't understand.'

'The look . . . staring into the distance . . . But do not take me seriously, my friend.'

It was a trait of his, to finish a sentence with a laugh, just as he did this time, after he'd observed something in me and made his point.

But what he'd said interested me. I wanted to know more, because now he had mentioned it I realised there was something that pulled me to the sea. To stare at it and reflect upon things as if there was some old consciousness staring back at me. Once, at the taverna, I'd heard a Greek-American who had returned to Ikaria for the first time in twenty years tell an old friend that the place had never moved on. '*Tempus stat*,' he said. 'Time stands still.'

It hadn't for me, suddenly remembering I was now thirty.

As I walked along the quayside, dawn's light had reached the hills above Aghios Kirikos, brightening the colours of the distant houses. I was carrying a bag full of barbunia and sardines. For some reason, Stelios had put a large crab in amongst them, the inedible sort we usually threw overboard. It had a red, grainy shell and black claws and peered at me with protruding eyes. It must have been Stelios's idea of a joke.

When I got back to Lefkada, I put the fish in Maria's fridge, which she was still happy for me to do, especially if it was barbunia. She'd add it to the menu as the 'Fresh Speciality of the Day'.

I walked back to the house and left the crab on the front doorstep, wanting to see how the children reacted to it. Ros had started teaching and so I hid behind the eucalyptus tree and listened in.

Sam was standing up reading from a book, speaking with good pronunciation about the fishing ports on the east coast of England. Somehow Ros was managing to keep Seth occupied painting watercolours that he seemed to finish every two minutes, showing them to Ros for her approval before starting another one. It is a gift, I thought, or a necessary skill a teacher has to possess, to keep children occupied. Ros certainly had it, and even when she saw me peeping around the tree she didn't allow herself to be distracted. I just blew her a kiss and became completely absorbed, watching the children being taught by their mother.

By the time they had finished their lesson, I had forgotten about the crab on the doorstep, until I heard Lysta scream.

'How on earth did that get here? It must have walked up from the beach,' I said, pretending to be completely mystified.

'Happy birthday, darling,' whispered Ros in my ear.

'It's not moving,' observed Sam.

'It's one of Dad's jokes,' said Ros.

'Well it's not funny, not funny at all,' said Lysta.

'I think it's dead,' stated Seth.

'Something else for your collection,' suggested Ros.

'Now,' I said, 'have you forgotten it is a big day in your father's life?'

'Happy birthday, Dad,' all three of them said together, and then they sang it to me.

'Mum's organised a party in the taverna and everyone's coming.'

'Yes, and Gregory's got a special present for you from Canada.'

'And Granny's going to telephone you at eight o'clock.'

'That's not all, Dad. We've got a present for you as well, even though you don't give us any pocket money.' From behind her back, Lysta brought out a parcel wrapped in newspaper and tied with some old string, obviously not wrapped up by Ros.

'A pair of sandals. Just what I've always wanted.'

Ros at last gave me some decent swimming trunks, and inside them a bottle of five-star Metaxa brandy.

Then I fell on the bed, the night catching up with me. Seth came over and tried to put my new sandals on my feet, while Lysta gave me a kiss. 'You smell of fish, Dad.'

'Thank you. Now come here and let me give you a big hug,' and they all jumped on top of me and in amongst them I managed to give Ros a kiss.

'And now I must sleep. I've been fishing all night.'

'Did you catch any barbunia?' It was the same thing Sam always asked me. I thought he liked saying the word more than he looked forward to eating it. It was a rather bony fish and Ros had to remove them all before he could take a mouthful.

I'd had four hours' sleep when I was woken by Paulo and Francesca calling from the veranda. I recognised what they were singing; 'Happy Birthday' has the same tune in any language. Whoever wrote it must have made a fortune in royalties.

I'd slept in my new swimming trunks, wanting to break them in.

'We have a little gift for you,' said Paulo, handing me a cassette tape and some rolled up toilet paper.

'Thank you,' I said. Toilet paper.

'Please open it.'

So I unrolled the sheets until I came to a joint.

'Some grass for you to smoke,' said Paulo.

'For you to get stoned,' added Francesca.

'That's very kind of you.'

I was in for quite an evening, what with the bottle of brandy as well.

'Did you get this from the same place, near the Toula Hotel?'

'Yes. There are three or four plants. We go and pick some whenever we want it.'

'It must be one of the workers.'

'Who knows, but there's plenty of it.'

'Whoever it is, they're watering it every day. The earth is always wet,' Paulo added.

'Why do you ask all these things?' said Francesca.

'I've heard the penalties are very stiff in Greece if you're caught with marijuana.'

The risks must have been minimal on Ikaria, though, with a police force of two who spent most of their time in cafés playing *tavli*.

'This is crazy,' said Paulo. 'In Italy if the police catch you with grass you get a fine, not sent to prison.'

As I walked to the monastery, I could see a Greek navy torpedo boat out on the Aegean, no doubt on its way to Samos. Another show of strength, but this time escorted by a helicopter that flew on ahead and then circled above. I never really knew the extent of the tension that existed between the two countries, only that the Ikarians believed they lived under the threat of a possible invasion. Vassili had told me it was nothing more than a flexing of military muscles and he thought there would not be another war. I hoped he was right.

Sister Ulita opened the gates and immediately led me round to the old outhouse. There were three donkeys, tethered together by a single rope to the bough of a cypress tree, each of them with a load of firewood on its back. On the way, Sister Ulita had been trying to explain something to me, but I couldn't understand anything other than *gaidaros*, which I knew was donkey.

Then an old man appeared pulling up his flies, wearing a straw hat that had seen better days. Sister Ulita ushered me towards him. He had no English but was friendly enough, and when he smiled I could count the teeth in his mouth. There were two, at the front.

We started to unload the logs and carry them into the outhouse, but what I thought was a job I was helping him with very quickly turned out to be mine alone. He walked off, or rather shuffled off, his shoes without laces, his heels worn down. It was difficult to fathom what went on between the islanders, for half an hour later, when I'd finished unloading the logs, I found him sitting with Sister Ulita at the courtyard table playing cards – and, it seemed, for money. What game they were engrossed in I did not know, but surely they were not gambling in the monastery? As I passed them, such was Sister Ulita's concentration she could only manage a half wave, and when I left all she said was, '*Avrio.*' Not like her at all.

🔳

Just as we were making our way to the taverna for my birthday evening, I could hear Maria shouting at the top of her voice, 'Neeko . . . Neeko, *ela, ela*, telephone. Where are you?'

It was Manos, Stelios's cousin.

'The potato boat is coming, yes? Five hundred drachma I pay you. Be here at midnight. Goodbye.'

He didn't give me a chance to tell him it was my birthday. I'd have to go, and I'd have to be sober, which was the hard part. Having to be disciplined while everyone around me raved on into the night.

When I told Gregory he said, 'That's cruel, man, so, so cruel. I'll come with you, if you want.'

I wasn't sure about that; I'd have to see what sort of condition he was in.

'Here,' he said. 'This is for you. Happy birthday.' He handed me a small parcel, which I undid, revealing a tin of maple syrup. *Sirop d'érable absolument pur* was written on the side.

'Absolutely pure maple syrup, man. My mother sent it over.'

'Thanks, Gregory. I've never had maple syrup before.'

'It's great stuff. A little bit of Canada for you.'

Maria gave me three kisses, one on each cheek, and a more sustained one on my forehead, saying '*Chronia polla, chronia polla*' which I took to be happy birthday.

Yannis shook my hand and informed me, 'You are still a boy,' which I was grateful to hear. He and Lottie had moved all the tables into an outer ring, to make a clear area where we could dance. Later in the evening a bouzouki player and two violinists were coming from the village of Christos.

At eight o'clock my mother rang and crackled happy birthday down the line. She said she could hear the noise coming from the taverna in Westbourne. Then Maria dropped a few plates, which smashed, and she thought some wild, debauched party was going on. She didn't get onto her favourite subject of when we were coming home, but said whenever that would be a present was waiting, which was a pullover she had knitted for me.

When I mentioned that I was not drinking and had to unload the potato boat from Samos at midnight, she reminded me I had a weak back and shouldn't be doing such work. A bit late to tell me that now. I told her all the news and that no, we had no plans to return to England. It was getting monotonous always having to reassure her the children were doing well with their school work.

Then the phone went dead and I sat down to eat the banquet that Maria and Lottie had prepared. Course after course of hummus, olives, Greek salads, souvlaki, cheeses and my favourite, barbunia. I'd finished my half-carafe of Ikarian wine and felt as if I hadn't had a drink at all. My stomach was pretty full, which helped; and Ikarian wine was only about eight per cent. So I ordered another half-carafe from Yannis. After all, it was my thirtieth birthday, a day that would never happen again.

While I was talking to him, Sarah came over and sat next to me with a neatly wrapped little parcel. On it was written *Happy birthday Nick, from Sarah* with three kisses. It was a book by John Cowper Powys called *Wolf Solent*.

'Sorry it's a bit battered, but I think you'll love it. It's set in Dorset and beautifully written,' she said.

'Thank you,' I said. I wanted to say more, because it was such a thoughtful gift. I could tell after reading just the first page how vividly it brought to life the countryside of my childhood.

Julia joined us. 'The only thing I can give you is this,' she said and throwing her arms around me kissed me full on the lips and held me there.

'That's how a Kiwi kisses . . . do you want another one?'

'Wow! Can I save it for tomorrow when I've recovered?'

'It's now or never.'

'Okay, now.'

'Hold your breath . . . here it comes.'

Ros told me I had another surprise coming. Lottie walked out into the centre of the taverna and announced she was going to sing a special birthday song for me. It was Cat Stevens's 'Wild World' and she sang it beautifully, unaccompanied. We all fell silent, mesmerised by her voice. Paulo and Francesca entwined themselves in some kind of erotic dance behind her, Francesca's hands moving up and down his body. Lottie didn't even know they were there; if she had, I am sure it would have finished her performance.

'Did you know she could sing like that?' I asked Gregory.

'Man, sometimes on the beach she sings a tune that's going around in her head, but that was something else.'

I wanted to talk to her, but didn't have a chance as Agathi and Vassili turned up carrying a birthday cake, quite a work of art. Amongst the white icing-sugar waves was a chocolate fishing boat that Agathi had made herself. Vassili gave me a traditional black fisherman's hat. Their children were relaxed enough in my company now to come and embrace me. Christos and Xenia had become close friends with Sam and Lysta, and whenever talk came up about when we would be going home it was those four who with one voice wanted us to stay for ever and go to the same school in Aghios Kirikos. Lysta never mentioned Eleri any more. For Leftari and Seth there was no such closeness, both living in their separate worlds.

'I think you should make a speech,' whispered Ros, 'especially as you'll be the first person to be leaving your own party.'

'That's not because I want to, and you're right.'

'Dad, let me smash some plates,' said Sam.

'Well, it's the custom, isn't it? Go on, then.'

Unfortunately the plate he dropped bounced and didn't break.

'Don't worry, Sam. I'll get everyone's attention,' I said, and stood on a table and shouted, 'Hello, can you hear me? *Kali spera*. First of all, a huge thank you to all of you! And the biggest of them to Maria and Lottie for laying on such a banquet. I'm sure there's no meaning to it and it's just a coincidence that our individual journeys have brought us all to Ikaria to spend a summer together, but I feel I have made some great friends. So let's not forget each other, and thanks again for tonight, all of you.'

'That was lovely,' said Ros. 'Where did it come from?'

'I don't know. I've never spoken a premeditated word in my life – oh, except once, when I gave that talk to the WI in

Bontnewydd. Do you remember?'

I should have known that the last person to arrive would be Datsun Jim, walking into the taverna with a goat on a rope. A kid to be precise, browny-black in colour; it refused to walk so he dragged it over to me.

'This is for you, to make your birthday happy.'

'Jim, that is kind of you, and *efkharisto* very much, but I cannot have a goat.'

'Of course, for the garden, and then you kill it.'

'Dad, let's keep it. Please. I'll look after it,' pleaded Lysta.

'No. I'm sorry, but the last thing we want is a pet goat.'

'You cannot say no, I give it to you as a friend.'

'Don't worry, Dad. I'll feed it every day,' said Sam.

'It doesn't need to be fed, we've got half of Ikaria growing in our back garden,' I said. 'And besides, it's a billy goat and not much bigger than a rabbit, and with everything so overgrown we wouldn't even see it.'

'Don't worry, I'll make sure it's looked after,' said Ros, knowing she'd be the one who would have to carry water to it every day.

'Jim, where is Thekla? Why is she not with you?'

'An accident. It is sad, she has twisted her foot, you know, very swollen.'

'You should go back and be with her.'

'Not now. Let's eat and dance.'

Then, as if on call, the musicians from Christos arrived and to start the dancing Ilias took Maria by the hand and began the slow traditional dance of Ikaria in the candlelit shadows. If that wasn't theatrical enough, a full moon had risen over the Aegean and, like a spotlight, enhanced the scene. Maria moved gracefully, bending her knees, stretching a leg out in front of her, clapping her hands above her head. It was remarkable for someone of her age and it was romantic.

I was fascinated by their sense of timing; it seemed to be an irregular beat that I couldn't tap my foot to, and yet they knew exactly when to take each coordinated step. Ilias was plainly a master, with elegance and a proud look, one moment back on his heels, clicking his fingers, the next suddenly lunging forward, swirling his whole body round, then slapping the ground with the palm of his hand. They danced as a couple and yet were separate, each absorbed in their own graceful movements. Then we all joined them and became Ikarians and danced in a large circle beneath the eucalyptus trees, arms on each other's shoulders, gently swaying.

As I sat down to finish what remained in my carafe of red wine, Ros asked me whether I was really going to unload the potato boat. It was already eleven o'clock.

'I must. We need the money.'

'I've got forty drachma,' said Sam, overhearing our conversation.

'That's my forty drachma, actually,' said Lysta. 'You lost a bet that I wouldn't dare eat an anchovy.'

'But you didn't eat it, you spat it out.'

'Mum, tell him, please.'

'Hey, man, when are we going?' asked Gregory.

'Let me start saying goodnight to everyone, then we should head off.'

The last thing I saw of my birthday party, as Gregory and I left the taverna, was Sarah and Ilias dancing the tango. It was nearly midnight, but I knew the boat wouldn't be on time; I just didn't know how late it would be. We weren't in any hurry, so Gregory produced a joint from his pocket and lit it, and in the warm starry night we smoked and chatted all the way into town. We'd always found it easy to talk to each other and so I told him that I thought Lottie could be easily hurt in the affairs of the heart.

'What are you trying to say to me?'

'I've got to know Lottie, that's all, and she's very fond of you. Don't forget she came here to recover from a broken heart. It would be cruel if she had to leave with it broken again.'

'I know that, and you're right. We'll talk . . . So what are you and Ros going to do?'

'I don't know. We've no plans to leave. I've never seen Ros so happy.'

Twelve thirty, and no sign of the potato boat, just as I had expected. Adonis was asleep in his lorry, a radio playing some Greek music that sounded like Nana Mouskouri.

A few yards further up the quayside under a flickering street lamp a group of teenagers were drinking, laughing and chasing one another. Amongst them I recognised Theo, revving up a motorbike with a girl sitting behind him, arms around his waist.

At one o'clock the overladen potato boat, deep in the water, spluttered into the harbour. Adonis woke up and came over and I introduced him to Greg.

'We work as before, Adonis.'

'*Ne*, with bollocks.'

Gregory had volunteered without realising just what he had let himself in for. He was flagging after half an hour, given the job of passing me the fifty kilo sacks, which I then lifted up on to the quayside. Sweat was pouring off him, dripping from his face, while the bearded skipper slept, as always, leaning back against the mast, this time without finishing his ouzo.

'I've got to take a break, man, I'm not as fit as you,' panted Gregory, who couldn't straighten himself up.

'*Korastika*,' I said.

'I'm knackered,' he said.

'That's what I said.'

And all the while Adonis had kept up with us, running each sack on a trolley up a ramp into the back of the lorry.

Three fifteen, and we'd unloaded about half the cargo, Gregory asleep amongst the sacks. Theo and his crowd were still on the quayside, blasting out music on a cassette player, racing their motorbikes past us. If Stelios had seen his brother now there would have been a fight. At last Adonis stopped to take a break, pouring a bottle of water over his head then drinking another one. He looked at Gregory, lost to the world.

'No balls,' he said.

At a quarter to six I lifted the last sack on to Adonis's trolley. The day was already bright, and fishing boats were leaving the harbour. Gregory stirred as the sun met his sleeping eyes. I'd had to roll him on to the deck to get to the last few sacks he'd been sleeping on.

'Man, I don't know how you do it.'

'Do what?'

'Such backbreaking work.'

'Come on, let's have a coffee and go for a swim.'

14

The Toula Hotel

It had been a long time since I'd spoken to Stamati, but this time I couldn't avoid him. I was sitting in a café in Aghios Kirikos when I saw him coming towards me, carrying a tray of baklava fresh from the bakery. I really didn't want to have to explain why I hadn't been to see him or visit his ageing mother, and I certainly didn't want to listen to all the unjustified, sickly stuff about how I had hurt him. But I knew he'd have the answers to some of my questions, so I waited while he put down his tray of baklava and pulled up a chair beside me.

'You know, I have given up on you now. My friendship is worth nothing to you.'

'You're right, Stamati, and your friendship is worth nothing to me,' I said dismissively. I wondered why I hadn't said it before. Then I asked him what I wanted to know: what was going on with Stelios? He looked visibly shaken by what I'd just said, but he told me Stelios was only fishing one day a week. The rest of the time he was taking tourists out to remote beaches, where they could swim and sunbathe. He was often at the nudist beach where the Germans liked to go and play naked badminton.

'But now he has a girl he's crazy about. She is from New Zealand, the other side of the world. And they try to keep it secret. She swims from the boat to Lefkada, not Aghios Kirikos, so no one will see them together. Then he is out with her in the evenings, taking her on his motorbike into the hills, and soon his wife will know everything. You cannot keep a secret for long in Aghios Kirikos.'

'How do you know all this?'

'Because I am his friend, and you are too, he has told me this. He is here today. Talk some sense into him.'

Now I knew why we were not fishing together any more. I was about to thank Stamati and be on my way before he could bring up his mother, but he had other ideas.

'I know you are working at the monastery for the sister, yes? And for this man Petros at the Toula Hotel?'

'You seem to know everything, Stamati.'

'This is a small island with many tongues, and I tell you to be careful of this man. He is trouble. There are many here who do not like him.'

'I'll remember that, but now I must go and find Stelios.'

It was obvious that the girl from New Zealand Stelios was crazy about was Julia. I had seen how well they got on when we went out that day with Theo. Although Sarah and Julia still shared a room at Lefkada, I hadn't seen a lot of them recently and they only occasionally joined us for supper.

It was late July and Aghios Kirikos was busy, very different from how it was on that cold February day when we first arrived. Greek-Americans who had houses on the island, and now Athenians too, were here with their families, the cafés nearly full of tourists. Children were fighting over ice creams from the freezer outside the kiosk, while old Ikarian men sat in their jackets and flat caps staring out to sea. Some fiddled with their *komboloi*, puffing on cigarettes hanging from their mouths. Others played *tavli*, oblivious of what was going on around them. It was the first time I had seen cars blocking the roads into the square. Donkeys weaved between them, bringing fruit in from the countryside, pulling carts full of *karpuzi*. Everywhere there were mopeds misfiring, waiters running in white aprons, carrying trays of drinks to the tables along the harbour front.

It appeared my hopes of being a fisherman were fading

away. I had tasted it and wanted it back. Everything I felt out in the Aegean had added a richness to my life. I was thinking about this as I walked towards the harbour, trying to understand what allowed a man to be swept away by his emotions. For that was what had happened to Stelios, capsized, you could say, by his love for Julia. And now he was being paid to take tourists out for the day instead of earning his living from doing what was in his blood, like his father and his grandfather before him.

Stelios was flat out, fast asleep on the boat, his head lying on a coil of rope, a denim cap pulled over his forehead. What you would have thought was a picture of contented peace. A lone seagull squawking on the mast did not disturb him. The boat was scrubbed clean with no nets or buckets in sight, none of the polystyrene floats that normally lay scattered around the deck. I got the impression that this cleanliness was the result of a woman's touch. When I jumped down and stood next to him, he stirred and propped himself up on his elbows, pushing his cap back on to his head.

The sun was fierce in his eyes, and as he clambered to his feet he yawned and leant over the side to scoop up handfuls of water to throw on his face.

'Ah, my English friend, how good it is to see you.'

'Stelios, what plans do you have?' I asked, skipping the niceties and not wanting to hear the excuses he'd make for not having told me where I stood.

'I am not fishing, my friend. I have other things to do, tourists to take out. Sometimes I make three thousand drachma a day. It is easy money, and for what? To lie on the beach with them, to swim with them . . . you understand how I feel?'

I raised my hands as a sign of acceptance. 'OK, Stelios. Let me know if anything changes.' There was nothing else I could say. I felt he could have shown me a little more consideration;

in fact, he hadn't shown me any. But as I turned to step up on to the quay he pulled me back.

'Look, my friend,' he almost whispered. 'There is more to it. You know it is dangerous for me.' He sighed, putting his head in his hands. 'It would be better for my life to be fishing with you.'

'I don't know what you mean.'

'The girl, Julia, you know her. She comes with me on the boat with the other tourists. OK, now I have told you.'

I was glad he had revealed his secret, rather than let me hear it from Julia. Besides, how long had we spent together, talking about our lives? Hadn't he once said to me he wouldn't fish with a man he didn't know? Not to tell me would have diminished everything we had gone through out on the Aegean. So I sat down on the other side of the boat and said nothing, letting my silence make the impact rather than having to trawl over his self-inflicted mess.

'Well, my friend, do you think I am a fool?'

I nearly said then what I had once said to Datsun Jim, 'Please don't keep calling me your friend', but I didn't, because I valued the time we had spent fishing together and didn't want to tarnish it. Still, 'friend' was a word some Ikarians used far too lightly.

It was Paulo and Francesca's last night. They were going on to Samos to meet up with a friend who had organised a gathering of anarchists from all over Europe. I could imagine what it would be like, complete chaos. But they had given Sam and Lysta a lot of attention, teaching them Italian, after a fashion, so it wasn't a total surprise when they gave me their address in Milan, wanting to keep in touch. I couldn't give them ours, because we didn't have one. I suddenly felt the weight of the future I was going to have to face up to.

Lysta had often asked Francesca if she could watch her put the safety pin through her nose. That last night, sitting in the taverna, she had her wish granted, which made us all squirm, but it was Paulo who gave Sam a lasting legacy. Whenever he had trouble with his school work, he told Ros he wanted to be an anarchist.

⌐

Lottie was now going to be working a twelve-hour day, and it made me realise just how long the taverna stayed open. Maria was up at seven, and in the summer people were still there after midnight, mostly Ikarians, who were never in a hurry to go to bed. It astonished me that Maria had the energy to keep it all going. Lottie made more money from tips than she was being paid, which showed just how good a waitress she was.

'Does it still feel like a holiday?'

'Yes, and Maria doesn't mind if I disappear every so often to go for a swim. But the place is never empty and I can't take a siesta.'

At least she was saving money; all her meals were free and, sleeping in a tent on the beach, life was cheap.

'Besides,' she said with a smile, 'I get to sleep with Gregory every night.'

Whether the affair would last beyond Ikaria I had no idea. Maria adored her and gave her and Gregory what she called 'the last supper' at the end of every evening, after the customers had left. Maria had a soft spot for Gregory as well, because he was always willing to help her by shifting crates of beer, unloading the drinks truck, and stacking bottles of Coke and Fanta by the kitchen door.

It was just as well I had been able to choose the hours I worked on the building site that would eventually become the Toula Hotel. When I'd done my stint, I'd go for a swim and wash the cement powder off me. Then, after a short break, I'd walk on to the monastery and reclaim my peaceful composure.

I had never seen Datsun Jim work so hard. He often shouted out 'Korastika!' to me, which made me laugh.

It was because of Zenas, the stocky, stubbled foreman, an unkempt individual who walked around the site with a whistle in his mouth. He blew it for the slightest reason, even a vehicle reversing nearby, though the warning seemed unnecessary as nothing moved at more than two miles an hour. We had found out he was a cousin of Petros, so had a vested interest in working us so hard. There was no let-up until we were allowed a fifteen-minute break at eleven o'clock, when everyone lit a cigarette, spat on the ground and rubbed the dust out of their eyes. It was like working in a chain gang; Zenas counted down the seconds, then blasted on his whistle when our time was up. Some of the bricklayers liked to take off their boots, and if they hadn't got them back on in the allotted time he gave them another blast.

He understood little English, so I could get away with being rude to him. When I said, 'Did you enjoy your last job as a prison guard?' he just looked at me vacantly. It made me feel better, until I realised he was watching me more closely than ever, seeing me as trouble.

Greek housing bricks were not as heavy as the ones back home, enabling the labourers to carry eight under each arm, climbing up ladders, stacking them in piles behind the bricklayers moving along the scaffolding boards. All the houses on the island would have been finished in a month if the Ikarians worked at this rate. But most of the workforce was from other islands, trying to make some money to send home.

There were many things we had to endure building the Toula Hotel, such as the wind that swept in from the Aegean swirling the dust, sticking our tongues to the roofs of our mouths. The only water supply came from a standpipe. It was unpleasantly warm to drink, so I just sipped enough to stop me getting dehydrated.

Petros always turned up at some time during the day in his BMW, overdressed and looking like a member of the Mafia. Zenas greeted him and the two of them strolled around with their hands behind their backs. Petros had a good command of English, and liked to show off to me. Whenever he walked past he would say something, usually carrying a hidden threat, such as 'Zenas tells me you are not a very fast worker'.

I just shrugged my shoulders at these remarks, rather than giving a verbal response. It was something ingrained in me from my time in the hills of Wales, when accusations were being chucked around over some dispute between neighbours. Shrugging your shoulders showed indifference. Not that I was indifferent to Petros, far from it, and I'd stand up to him if necessary. He was an arrogant businessman who didn't give a damn about how unpopular he was, money being the only thing that mattered to him. But I also needed to keep the job.

'There are more labourers coming on the ferry tomorrow,' he told me.

'Hope you'll have enough wheelbarrows in that case,' I replied.

He cast a glance at Zenas, who I could tell had not thought of that, and they walked off exchanging words, Zenas scribbling something in a notebook.

Sister Ulita greeted me in a state of anxiety, grabbing hold of my cuff, pulling me with some urgency to follow her. I had not seen her like this before and I thought something serious must have happened as we hurried across the courtyard. Maybe the goats had got out and wreaked havoc. But there they lay, quietly chewing the cud under the olive trees, getting to their feet as we passed. We hurried on, past the beehives and into the vegetable garden, up the steep slope to the sluice gate and beyond to a small hidden door in the boundary wall of the monastery, which we could only get through on our hands and knees. I got to my feet in an area I had not been to before, out in the scrub with the smell of wild thyme spicing the air.

We walked a few yards until below us I could see a stream of pure water running along a gully before it disappeared underground. I realised this must be where the monastery's water came from, but I still didn't know what Sister Ulita wanted to show me. We walked further, to where the gully widened and the water flowed more strongly, and there lay some pickaxes and shovels. Stones had been cleared and what looked like some exploration work had begun.

'*Panagia!*' she said, raising her arms to the heavens. I didn't understand why she was so upset and I knew she couldn't explain. It was one of those frustrating times when I felt inadequate because I couldn't speak the language. How could I help her if I didn't know what was wrong?

When we returned to the monastery, she hid herself away for the rest of the day, leaving Artemis and me to have lunch together in the courtyard. A strange unease had come over the place, not helped by Artemis, who didn't bother to lay for the unexpected visitor in Sister Ulita's absence. It showed me what she thought of her friend's beliefs, as it was something the nun insisted upon. I suggested we should lay two more places in case Sister Ulita did decide to join us.

'You will not see the sister again today, and neither will the unexpected visitor arrive,' she said indignantly. I didn't care for her attitude, so I laid the two places myself.

'If you want to keep on believing in outdated ancient customs that's up to you,' she snapped, before storming off to fetch a bottle of wine. 'If it will make you happy, I will be the unexpected visitor.' She sat down at the end of the table.

'What has brought about your bad mood?'

She didn't answer straight away, concentrating on removing the cork. 'She gets hysterical. It's always the same when they come to steal the water.' She filled her glass, drank it and then poured herself another one. It was the first time I'd seen her have wine with her lunch. 'And now she will stay in her room, and in the morning she will not speak, and I am fed up with it.'

Artemis was going to get drunk. She told me about the history of the water wars, as she called them, the long-standing battles with the islanders over the fresh water that flowed to Aghios Kirikos from the land owned by the monastery. But it was not the past that was upsetting Sister Ulita. It was the new threat that Petros posed with the building of the Toula Hotel.

A half-bottle of wine later, she began to eat, picking at the salad leaves, soaking up the olive oil with her bread.

'I wanted to ask you, why was Sister Ulita playing cards with the old man who brought the firewood?'

'He comes every year and they play an old Ikarian card game. If she wins, she does not pay for the wood.' She took another sip from her glass. 'So come on, talk to me . . . pretend I am the unexpected visitor. Let us begin our little game.' She pushed the bottle in my direction.

I could never act out a part. Even in the school play I'd been unable to remember my lines.

'So we find ourselves together in a monastery. Why are we here? And what are we going to do, the two of us? Have you thought about that?'

'I don't know what I'm meant to be saying.'

'You would like to make love to me, wouldn't you?' She took the wine bottle back, running her finger up and down it before she looked at me and said, 'We cannot make love in a monastery where invisible eyes are looking down on us.'

Her frustration spilt over then.

'I have many English swear words, angry ones that would tell you how I feel.'

'Swear as much as you want, Artemis.'

'I am here to embroider the altar cloth, because I made a promise to the bishop, nothing more than that. So if you are not going to play this game, go, otherwise I will curse you.'

So I left her and went off to do my work in the gardens, unable to shake off the feeling of gloom in what was a glorious afternoon. I kept thinking about Sister Ulita, and about Artemis, while everything around me was just the same as it ever was, busy with butterflies, swallows fizzing through the air. It was strange how the heat altered the perception of time, the minutes slow as I worked under the cloudless sky, detached from my surroundings, with the relentless sound of the cicadas.

⌐⌐

It was the only time I had walked through the courtyard and left the monastery without seeing either Artemis or Sister Ulita. The shutters were closed across the windows of their sleeping quarters. The remains of our lunch had not been cleared away; amongst the plates stood the empty wine bottle, and flies were buzzing around the salad.

I was all at sea as I walked back to Lefkada. Artemis disturbed my emotions; I'd never met a woman like her and I didn't know what was going on. And I realised that perhaps I was getting too closely involved in the lives of others – in too deep you could say.

It was only when Lysta came running towards me shouting that Gregory was showing off, trying to balance on a *karpuz*i, that I felt I had returned to my familiar world. I was home again.

15

All About Water

Early August and Gregory the Gregarious, who had been here nearly two months, said he couldn't remember a single day of rain. Yet when the wind blew the dust off the fig trees by the road the leaves were still bright green. The grapes were now beginning to turn purple in the sun, the olive groves growing heavy with fruit. The peaches that I brought from the monastery, which we ate with goat's yoghurt, were large and juicy and a particular treat for Lysta, who lived mostly on aubergines and every kind of green bean grown on the island. It had concerned us to have a child so fussy about what she ate. At least after watching the nun making so many cheese dishes, she had added these to her diet. But for all of us, the food from the monastery was fresh and delicious and the children always asked for more.

Since Gregory had taught Sam how to tell the time he'd become a sort of uncle, telling our son great stories about life in Canada, how cold the winters were, how heavy with snow. He invited us to visit him when he returned home to Montreal. We sat around a table in the taverna and he passed his camera to Sam, who took a picture of Ros and me, his first ever photograph. Then Gregory took a family snap and promised he would send it to us. Sam asked him what Ros and I had also been wondering: whether Lottie would be going with him.

'Who knows, man? Not me.'

But there was something in the air that evening, about making decisions, the talk mostly of home, picking up the threads of our lives again. Sarah was having to face up to a few things: returning to England, taking up her place at university. I couldn't tell what was going through her mind. Was the affair with Ilias just a holiday romance that she had already sorted out with herself, or was there more to it? What was going to happen between Julia and Stelios when the summer came to an end? Living on Ikaria had disconnected us from the outside world.

Ros said we would have to decide soon: do we stay, or do we go and take on the future, whatever it may be? I had been waiting for her to raise the subject. She clearly loved the Ikarian way of life, and of course her friendship with Agathi had influenced her. They had already talked about the possibility of the children's attending the school in Aghios Kirikos and Ros teaching English there. But when I asked Agathi if Ros would be paid she wasn't sure, saying the school relied on donations from pupils' families to keep it going.

Did we really want to spend a winter here, without electricity, wearing our socks under heaps of blankets? We already knew what the island was like in February; it could be a lonely place when the sun wasn't shining. However, I still felt we hadn't yet run our course on Ikaria. But Ros and I agreed that by the end of the month a decision would have to be made.

᠄

It was the first anniversary of Elvis's death, 16 August 1978. Not that I had realised, until I heard the radio on the beach playing his songs. The first record I ever bought was 'Hard Headed Woman', in 1958. I saved up my pocket money for it, all seven shillings and sixpence. I used to lie in my bedroom playing it again and again. My mother, having heard it enough, made me keep my door shut. Now here I was singing it to myself as I waded into the Aegean to wash off the day's work at the Toula.

As I walked out of the water, I noticed Sarah sitting on the beach deeply engrossed in a letter she was reading.

'Not bad news, I hope?'

'You startled me . . . no, not really. Most of it's good.'

'You look unhappy,' I said.

'I was thinking about my father. As you know he's a dairy farmer, worried about the price of milk.'

I changed the subject, wanting to cheer her up. 'Have you had a good day with Ilias?'

'I've never had a day like it. I've been cracking open almonds with a pestle, hundreds of them, helping his mother.'

'Do you get on well with her?'

'I think she might see me as a future daughter-in-law.'

'Oh? Are things that serious?'

'I just don't know.'

'But you are staying in Ikaria?'

'I'm trying to decide what I should do. I feel pulled in so many directions.

'Anyway, I'm looking forward to this evening. There's a big family gathering and Ilias has promised to play the spoons, that sort of American hillbilly music, which he does brilliantly. He tried to teach me after all the hours on the almonds, but I was useless. There's a real skill to it.'

5.

That evening, Angelos appeared at the taverna. I had seen him working on the Toula site, covered in dust and cement powder like everyone else, but I'd never been able to speak to him; difficult with Zenas forever watching us, with that bloody whistle in his mouth. He was young and dark with a thickening beard and brown eyes. He looked like Cat Stevens, in fact so like him, he would have passed as his double. He finished his Amstel in one long, thirst-quenching gulp, leaving a white frothy moustache above his dark beard. His English was good and he told me he was a student at Athens University, studying engineering, and had come here for work. He was penniless, and Ikaria, where you could sleep on the beach and pick fruit from the trees, was a cheap island to survive on. He was working ten hours a day for Petros and would not leave until he had saved thirty thousand drachma. That's how much he needed to get through the winter back in Athens. He thought Petros drove everybody too hard and was a fool to deduct pay for being just five minutes late.

'He would get more out of us if he softened his attitude instead of being a bully.'

Angelos had heard that a JCB was arriving on the ferry soon to dig a trench that would bring water to the hotel.

'Where will this water come from?' I asked him anxiously.

'From some old monastery two kilometres away. I'm not sure of the exact location.'

Ros came over to say the children were hungry and she wanted to order some supper. I was about to introduce her to Angelos when she smiled and said, 'Hello. Has anyone ever told you you look just like Cat Stevens?'

'I'd had the same thought,' I said.

'A few people have told me that. It's a pity I don't have his voice and can't play the guitar.'

I asked him if he wanted to join us, but he was eating in Aghios Kirikos that night.

Over supper, I told Ros how I was getting involved in a Greek drama that was unfolding around us. It was all about water, something we took for granted, but the lack of which could bring out the worst in people. And the Toula Hotel would need a lot of it, with a hundred bedrooms, a restaurant and a swimming pool. Petros had no right to take the monastery's water and, as Ros knew, I couldn't stand by and do nothing to help Sister Ulita.

Datsun Jim's metamorphosis was ongoing. When I met him the next day with a trowel in his hand laying bricks, I was quite astonished. He had shaved off his beard and looked ten years younger. We managed to grab two minutes before Zenas appeared. He told me that on 1 October he would be marrying Thekla, up in the hills in the village of Mounte. I asked him how many people he was going to invite but he didn't understand. Apparently on Ikaria whoever wanted to just turned up for the celebrations. Everybody, it seemed, invited themselves.

As I worked, I couldn't stop thinking about the whole Toula Hotel project. There were so many things I didn't understand. Did Petros have planning permission, or was it required in the first place? What deals had been done? Could an Athenian businessman legally divert water for a hotel he was building? I needed to speak to Artemis, who could translate Sister Ulita's side of the story. Was there no law to protect the monastery? But nothing was likely to happen until the digger arrived, whenever that might be. *Avrio*, no doubt, and *avrio* could be a long time on Ikaria.

Already, as I walked from Lefkada, I could tell we were in for an extremely hot day. For the past week, temperatures had been in the high eighties. I'd not been on the road for long when I saw two people coming towards me and recognised Sarah and Ilias.

'What are you two doing out so early? I don't often meet anyone on my way to the monastery.'

'We went to the *panagiri* in Arethousa last night,' said

Sarah, 'which was amazing, but the bus broke down on the way back.'

'Have you been walking half the night?'

They had, and although Ilias knew the old drovers' tracks it had still taken them four hours.

'It was the most wonderful walk. Not the easiest in sandals, but I'll never forget it. We met an old lady in one of the deserted villages who seemed to be the only inhabitant. She's a distant relative of Ilias's and gave us some raki to drink.'

'You must be exhausted.'

'We are,' said Ilias. 'We're going for a swim at the hot springs and then we'll sleep.'

Artemis had never opened the door to me when I arrived at the monastery, but she did that morning. Sister Ulita was on the telephone and would be for some time.

'She is organising the troops, is how I think you say it in English.'

'Is she speaking to the police?'

'No, not the police, to the bishop of Samos.'

'Will he come to Ikaria and sort out Petros?' I asked.

'How do you know this?'

'Because it is he who needs the water.'

But she wouldn't talk about it, as if she had something else on her mind.

'I have told you, I am here to embroider the altar cloth for the celebrations on Saint Adrianos's day.' And it appeared that the matter was closed as far as she was concerned. 'Do you know how to kill rats?' she asked bluntly.

'There's Perseus. A cat should be enough.'

'You mean the overfed animal who lies around sunbathing all day? Is this one of your jokes?'

I could hear the nun on the telephone, but it was hard to tell her mood, because Greek always sounded to me like a language in a hurry, dramatic even when the subject was something trivial. When she eventually appeared, her sunglasses reflecting the cypress trees, she seemed in a much better state than when I last saw her. Maybe help was coming from Samos.

All Artemis wanted to do was tell her about the rat, pointing to where she had seen it run into the stonework outside the pantry where the food was kept. Sister Ulita disappeared and came back with Perseus and pushed his nose into the hole, but as soon as she put him down he wandered off, not showing the slightest interest.

'You see, the animal is useless.'

When we met for lunch and Sister Ulita prayed, as she always did before our first mouthful, Artemis sat impatiently, looking agitated. If Sister Ulita knew how exasperated her friend was feeling she ignored it.

We were all surprised when the bell rang out in the courtyard. I'd not heard it before within the monastery, and the sound of it echoed from wall to wall. Sister Ulita immediately raised both hands to her cheeks and got into an excited flap, sending Artemis to the kitchen to bring more food and pouring water into the unexpected guest's glass. Then she ran to open the gates and we heard her cries of joy. It wasn't one unexpected guest that appeared but four of them: Ros and the children. I was surprised they had suddenly turned up uninvited, until Ros whispered to me that she hoped their visit might take Sister Ulita's mind off the troubles she was facing.

Artemis quietly left the table without acknowledging anyone. I thought perhaps she didn't like children; she was clearly not the motherly type, and I could imagine them annoying her. Lunch went on for over an hour, without any let-up from the cicadas. The sun glistened on the church bell, while a lizard stood perfectly still on the flagstones, as if listening to every word we said.

Sister Ulita only ever got out her phrase book if she had an important point to make, usually to do with the children. She thought Sam was tall for his age; eventually, after much patience and thumbing through almost every page, she said Seth lived in a world of dreams, '*Oneiro, oneiro.*' He did indeed; Ros and I nodded in agreement.

When Sister Ulita went for her siesta, I suggested to Ros that before they left we should go and pick some peaches and pears that were ripening every day now in the orchard. I had to lift each of the children up to reach the branches, and once we'd filled a basket we sat in the shade for a while. The scent of the warm peaches made it impossible not to eat some, the juice running down our chins and through our fingers. We watched the monastery chickens scratching in the dry earth, shaking out their feathers. Butterflies settled on leaves and dragonflies zipped through the quivering heat haze. It really did feel like the Garden of Eden.

After Ros and the children had gone home I climbed the steep steps of the vegetable garden and sat for a while. Out in the Aegean, a large yacht was passing on its way to Samos. I saw them every now and then but they never stopped at Ikaria; there was nothing for their millionaire owners here. Overhead, a Greek air force jet, no doubt showing off its military capabilities, flew towards the mountains and disappeared, its noise shattering the peace.

I realised how closely we had become entwined in the lives of others, and how all the kindness and hospitality so many Ikarians had shown us had made us feel at home. If I had been a different person and kept everything at a distance I wouldn't have cared so much about what was taking place. How little control one has over outer events that pick you up and drag you along.

I knew Maria was in her seventies, but her son, Dinos, whom she had mentioned to me before, could only have been in his thirties. So she must have had him late; what my mother called an afterthought, and others called an accident. She introduced me to him when he arrived, a tall, gangly young man. I could see the family resemblance, the same thin build as Yannis.

Every summer he came back from Athens where he worked in a museum, cataloguing artefacts. Like many Greeks, he was fluent in English, and when we talked he told me I would be seeing a lot of him in the taverna, fighting with his mother over who should do the cooking.

'Don't be worried if you hear us arguing in the kitchen,' he said. 'We disagree a lot over our recipes.'

'But I like your mother's cooking, especially the squid in olive oil.'

'Ah yes, but how can she fry chips in goat fat! If I were not a historian I would have been a chef.' I didn't dare tell Lysta about those chips. His speciality was a traditional Ikarian dish called *soufico*, usually made from aubergines, courgettes, peppers and tomatoes.

'Hey, maybe one night I could cook this for you.'

It was the first time I had arrived on site and not found Datsun Jim already laying bricks. He was usually there at seven and liked to get a spurt on before the sun got too high, when the sweat ran down our backs and our T-shirts clagged under our armpits. Since being with Thekla, he had always been punctual. But Zenas just moved me on to mix cement for another bricklayer, building a high wall of breeze blocks that was probably going to be the main entrance.

Angelos was working nearby, driving a dumper truck full of heavy electric cables. He waved me over and said we urgently needed to talk in our fifteen-minute break. Petros was there early, walking around a marked-off area to the side of the hotel where I was sure they were going to build the swimming pool. How many gallons would that take to fill, never mind showers and baths? I was becoming quite obsessed with the whole water situation.

At eleven Angelos told me everyone was fed up with their pay and conditions. They wanted at least another thirty drachma an hour, which was about enough to buy a newspaper and a packet of chewing gum. They had elected him as their spokesman, because he went to university. He was reluctant to fulfil this role, being only twenty years old, and thought Petros would just laugh and sack him on the spot.

'There must be a way to achieve what we want,' I said.

Then Zenas blew his whistle and the break was over without anything being decided.

'Let's meet at the taverna tonight,' I said.

At that moment Datsun Jim drove at speed onto the site and rushed over to Zenas. He apologised profusely for being late, with all the exaggerated gestures that Ikarians used to drive home their point. To make up the time, he didn't stop for his half-hour lunch break. Later in the afternoon, Zenas moved me back to work with him, and I finally heard about his troubled morning. His wife-to-be had found his adult magazines. Jim had moved them from under the passenger seat of the pick-up and thought they'd be safe hidden beneath the straw bedding in the goat hut. On an unexpected visit, Thekla came upon the goat not chewing the cud but eating a girlie magazine. And, to make matters worse, she discovered several more, half-chewed, beneath the straw. Jim was dejected and didn't know where he stood with her.

Angelos and I had our arranged rendezvous in the taverna. It felt like the meeting of two collaborators secretly planning the downfall of a despotic dictator. That was certainly our intention, if Petros didn't give everyone a wage increase and improve the working conditions by providing lavatories and washing facilities. Whenever someone was caught short they had to take themselves off into the scrub. I told Angelos workers went on strike all the time in England, but they did have trade unions to do their fighting for them, which was unheard of on Ikaria, because there was no workforce. Everyone who worked was self-employed and agreed a price man to man; I doubted anyone paid taxes. It was a cash economy, reinforced by the exile of the communists to Ikaria during the civil war.

The weakness was obvious. Petros's labourers were not a collective group of men who spoke with one voice, but poor individuals who came from other islands and sent what they earned back to their dependent families. Lots of Ikarians survived on the money they received from relatives who worked in the United States. The merchant ships were full of Greeks. Husbands left their wives and children, sometimes for years, to keep them all fed.

As we sat talking, it became obvious that Angelos was not the person to confront Petros. He didn't have the hardness needed to stand up to a tyrant, in fact he was an extremely likeable human being. Petros would throw him off site as soon as he tried to negotiate. Then he'd threaten everyone with the sack unless they returned to work. I suggested he'd be less comfortable dealing with an Englishman, not knowing how I would react to his threats.

'I'll take him on if you will do the translating.'

'You are a brave man.'

'No, I'm not. I've just got far less to lose than you.'

In three days' time, we decided, we would spring a few surprises on Petros, catch him off guard, we weren't yet sure how. Another Amstel might help.

I told Ros what we were planning. She said I shouldn't get involved in the island's politics and ought to let them fight it out amongst themselves. But I was already involved, not only working on the Toula Hotel, but committed to the monastery as well. She was concerned about the possible consequences for the future, if we were going to continue living on Ikaria. What she didn't know was that I had reached a decision about staying on the island. It had come to me after talking to Vassili again. The winter on Ikaria was like a hibernation, and finding work to pay our way would be impossible. Relying on the generosity of the islanders was out of the question. I knew all of us would love to stay, but practicalities made the decision inevitable. Ros and I needed to talk.

16

The Showdown

It was a quiet August evening and Gregory asked if I would go for a walk with him. The light was sharp on the horizon's edge but the intense blue of the sea no longer reflected the sun. Clouds were floating up over the mountains. He had a handful of figs and offered me one which I declined. The pips got stuck in my teeth. But I liked watching how he peeled off their skins symmetrically in neat little strips. I'd noticed his dexterity before, when he changed the film in his camera, and because I didn't possess such skills it left an impression on me. I had a feeling this was going to be a man-to-man talk.

'I suppose there is nothing quite like it, wandering through a long hot summer living half naked on a beach, waking yourself up with an early morning swim in the Aegean, having a girl by your side and not noticing time passing because life is so simple. If only the world could stand still.'

That's what Gregory was thinking, now the end was in sight. That and just how difficult it was going to be to leave Ikaria. Suddenly the days were numbered, his summer becoming full of yesterdays. He talked while we skimmed stones. I suggested he put a date on his departure and tell Lottie, so she could prepare for it and make her own plans.

I didn't find out whether this was helpful, because we were distracted by the sight of a girl diving into the sea from a fishing boat. I knew that boat. It was Stelios's, and the girl swimming to shore was Julia, returning no doubt from a stolen day in one of the remote coves that could only be reached by sea. As she stepped onto the stony beach in a white bikini, twisting the water from her hair, she was completely unembarrassed, smiling and pleased to see us.

'Hi, guys! God, how I love this country, being out on the sea. It reminds me of New Zealand, where I grew up in the Sounds of the South Island. So beautiful, the same rugged landscape and bright light.'

'Do you miss it?' I asked.

'Oh, yes, and I'll go back one day, but there's so much to see and do on this side of the world. And what a day it's been! Most of it on a sandy beach all to ourselves. We cooked fish over an open fire. Stelios is a passionate man all right, and boy can he sing.'

'You're quite a girl, Julia,' said Gregory. 'Come on, let's go and have a beer.'

🔳

Angelos was waiting for me at the taverna, anxious to hear my plan, which I had worked out the night before, drinking a glass of Ikarian wine on the patio, while Ros and the children slept. Despite the three slow-burning insect repellent coils I'd lit, the mosquitoes had decided to make a meal of me.

Time does not go on the same for ever, the days uniformly following one another, the sun always rising into a cloudless sky, change never visible on the horizon. And now I felt a nervous energy: I was not only playing a part, I was interfering in the life of the island that had been our home for the past seven months.

'The art of surprise is a great advantage in unnerving your enemy,' I told Angelos. We should all meet at the entrance to the site, and I'd state our demands to Zenas. Then we would wait for Petros to turn up, and confront him as a united band of brothers.

'It will only work if we stand together and no one weakens.'

'What if he refuses and loses his temper?'

'Then we all sit down. Tell everyone we need to hold out for three days. Then he will give in. He's got a hotel to build.'

'You are sure about this?' he said, as if he doubted me.

'Of course. I have seen it many times in England. Yes, there will be angry words, but everyone will calm down eventually and reach an agreement and we will all return to work.'

'You make it sound so easy.'

'We must not weaken,' I repeated, asking Angelos what the Greek was for 'hold your nerve' and telling him it should become our slogan. I had a feeling I would be saying it a lot over the next few days.

Ros was reluctantly playing her part by agreeing to milk the goats when I couldn't, but she warned me again that I had no idea what I was letting myself in for.

'There's no hospital on the island, you know,' were her last words on the matter.

Gregory the Gregarious gave me his opinion too. He thought Petros would retaliate by attacking the weakest, and so frightening the others. He didn't think we had a chance of victory.

'If things get out of hand we'll call the police,' I said. 'All two of them.'

'It's highly likely that Petros has already paid them off,' said Gregory, putting an end to that option.

We would just have to wait and see what happened.

🔁

At the end of each day, as I was about to leave the monastery, Sister Ulita would put my wages into a basket. Today I could see they included a honeycomb, straight from the hive, which she had wrapped in greaseproof paper. She beckoned me to come and sit with her at the table in the courtyard, and Artemis joined us. Sister Ulita took a handwritten note from her pocket and read silently to herself before passing it to Artemis, who smelt of cigarette smoke. Artemis cleared her throat and said, 'The sister has asked me to translate this for her.'

The note explained the troubles with the islanders over the water. The matter had never been resolved and now Sister Ulita had to deal with the new threat from Petros and the Toula Hotel. I remembered then when she had taken me to see what was happening up above the vegetable garden, outside the monastery wall. However, troops were on their way, meaning fifteen nuns were coming from Samos, and they would help her resist Petros.

'What has all this got to do with me?' I asked, looking at Sister Ulita.

'You must stand guard for us until our friends arrive from Samos,' Artemis insisted. 'You will do this for the sister.'

It dawned on me then that of course they didn't know I was working at the Toula Hotel. How would I ever be able to explain that it was just a job? I knew they would see it as an act of betrayal. But my loyalties were split now, between the monastery and my fellow labourers; it was getting complicated.

'I will come when I can in the morning,' I said, 'and return in the afternoon as I always do, until the nuns arrive from Samos.'

🔲

We all gathered at the site entrance, watching Zenas undo the padlock to let us in, but when we just stood there and no one followed him through, he smelt trouble.

'*Ela, ela,*' he shouted, beckoning us forward, but not a single one of us moved. He blew his whistle repeatedly and threw his arms about, but we all stayed where we were and watched him.

Then I walked casually out of the crowd, taking my time to come face to face with him. I was taller than Zenas, who was stocky on his short legs, thick in the thighs. He was at least two stone heavier than me, but I had the height, and he was put at a disadvantage by having to aim his aggression up at me. Which he did anyway, shouting in Greek. I asked Angelos to translate what he was ranting on about. It was just as I suspected: we would all be sacked without pay as soon as Petros arrived.

'I don't think so,' I said calmly, slightly overacting, but he got the message that we were not going to enter the site and so turned his attention to the workforce. It didn't take long for him to see he was getting nowhere. He jumped into the site pick-up and would have driven straight into us if we hadn't leapt out of the way. It took literally ten minutes for the dust to settle.

I noticed the key was still in the padlock, so I closed and locked the gates. No one could get in now, and that included Petros, unless he had a pair of wire cutters.

'Hold your nerve,' I said to everyone.

'*Kratiste tin psychraimia sas*,' echoed Angelos.

Then as we all began to sit down Datsun Jim drove up, unshaven, with Coke stains down the front of his T-shirt, the dishevelled Jim of old who looked as if he had spent the night in a goat hut. He seemed not to notice the scene that surrounded him and came straight over to me, slapping his forehead as if he was fed up with everything.

'I've had enough, no more women. It's over with Thekla.'

'Sorry to hear that, Jim, but things are a bit difficult here. We're on strike.'

'Strike? What does this word mean?'

'It means we have stopped work.'

'Why didn't you tell me?'

'I've just told you.'

'About women. You are married to one, you must have known.'

'It's true I am married to a woman, but we can't talk now. Later,' I said, putting a consoling arm on his shoulder. 'Now you must join us. We are refusing to work; we are on strike.'

'I will work. Do not worry, my friend.'

'*Ochi*, Jim, you must not work. Do you understand?'

At which point Zenas returned, repeatedly sounding his horn, trying to intimidate us, swerving the pick-up from side to side. When he reached the gates and found them locked he searched frantically in his pockets for the key, and then realised he was shut out. A minute later Petros arrived. He chose a more dignified approach, walking in front of us in his dark suit, like a predator stalking its prey. I moved quickly and stepped up in front of him. Although I was playing a dangerous game, I wanted to show the others I wasn't afraid.

'Petros, we need to talk.'

He pushed up his sunglasses and gave me a look of intense anger, unable to get a word out, or least not a word of English, which needed some thinking about. To try to articulate the anger he felt in a foreign language would weaken his position. For a brief moment I had the upper hand, and he said, 'What do you want?'

So I told him our demands. When he'd heard what I had to say he turned his back on me, laughing theatrically. Zenas, his obsequious minion, echoed the hollow laughter as they walked away and began whispering to each other.

Suddenly Petros swung around and addressed me.

'What has this got to do with you, who doesn't even belong here, a tourist who has overstayed his welcome? You should leave Ikaria and go back to England.' He gesticulated as if slapping me with the back of his hand.

'You won't get rid of me that easily. You should consider what we have asked for, and what you are going to do about it.'

'Nothing. I will sack you all and bring others to work here.'

'Not if we stay here and block the entrance.'

He punched the wire mesh as his temper boiled over, then got into his BMW and drove off, leaving Zenas in the pick-up, like a man trapped without a friend in the world. After glaring at us fiercely, but to no effect, he left too.

We sat there for most of the day, all of us except Datsun Jim, who promised to return within one hour. I held out little hope of seeing him again now he was alone once more to fend for himself. His brother Giorgos had returned to America and he would slip back into his old ways. I had no idea what he thought about our situation. I was sure it didn't make any difference to Jim who he was working for, except that he had always done a full day for Petros, no doubt because Thekla kicked him out of bed each morning. I felt a painful sympathy for him, because without a guiding hand he was lost.

But he was also unpredictable, for suddenly he returned with Maria and her son in the back of the truck. He and Dinos then lifted out crates of Amstel and Coca-Cola, while Maria passed among the workforce like Mother Teresa, handing out fruit to everyone.

The apprehensive mood we had been in all morning took on a more optimistic air with this unexpected welcome twist. Maria, I knew, would stand up to anyone, and Dinos shared his mother's fighting spirit. He stood in the back of the pick-up and made a rousing speech, of which I didn't understand a single word, but Angelos translated. It wasn't about the demands we were making, but about how the Toula Hotel would ruin the landscape and the island did not have the necessary utilities to provide for such a large construction. He went on, about sewerage and, of course, the water supply. It was all true, and the more I listened the more I realised that the battle being fought here had spread beyond the rights of a few workers to something far greater, to whether the islanders wanted the Toula Hotel to be built at all. I had done my bit and could now step back. Dinos was the man to take this forward and defeat Petros.

Nobody could have known what was about to follow. For moving at no more than five miles an hour along the coastal road came a JCB digger, a black and yellow leviathan with giant rubber tyres, spitting up stones behind it, giving out a dense black smoke. It swung its great shape towards us and ploughed through the gates, flattening them as if they had been held together with paper clips.

Then Petros reappeared in his BMW and stood in front of the digger.

'What would you do in his position?' I asked Dinos. He thought the man had two choices, either to concede and meet our demands, or to sack everyone and bring in a new workforce, which could take days. And where would he find them? Certainly not on Ikaria. He would have to bring them from other islands, Samos or maybe Mykonos. If this was his course of action, we would have no alternative but to stand at the gates each morning and stop them coming on site. I knew this was impossible: none of us could fight a long, drawn-out battle because we all lived hand to mouth; we could survive until the end of the week, then everything would fall apart. We needed to frighten Petros into immediate submission.

Then I had one of those inspirational moments, when the solution to the whole conflict suddenly came to me. We should gather Ikarians to stand shoulder to shoulder with us and demostrate our solidarity. We could bring them out of the bars and cafés of Aghios Kirikos, and show a united front. It made sense, even if most of them probably knew little about the hotel.

For the rest of the day we played football, or went swimming, or threw prickly pears high into the air, trying to catch them with our bare hands; anything to stave off boredom. As the afternoon dragged on, Dinos and I talked. He was more than happy to drum up support from his cousins in Aghios Kirikos. All those cousins, I thought to myself. Where else would you look first, but within the extended family?

Sarah and Julia abandoned their lovers for the evening and joined us for Gregory the Gregarious's last night on Ikaria. It had come as a complete surprise when he'd told us he'd decided he wasn't returning to Montreal, but was making his way to Africa. Lottie was leaving too, going back to Amsterdam after spending a few days with him in Athens before he flew to Cairo.

I'd miss him and hoped we'd keep in touch. I wrote down my mother's address in England and stuffed it into his shirt pocket. We'd become fond of Lottie too and they both had taken to the children, who expressed their feelings by begging them to come and stay with us wherever that would be. Seth gave Gregory his most prized possession, the corpse of a large black beetle wrapped up in a paper napkin.

I thought we probably wouldn't see Gregory again. Friends can fade away and be quickly forgotten when the world opens up. And that would certainly be the case for Gregory, travelling into deepest Africa. Maria planted a kiss on his forehead, insisting he return next year. Yannis, not given to showing his emotions, actually embraced him.

As for Maria's farewell to Lottie, she burst into tears. She had been a great help to her for the last few months.

Dinos gathered us together to take a photograph, capturing a split second in our lives, smiling, our arms round each other, glasses raised. Then Gregory suggested we go for one last swim.

In the early September moonlight we dived through waves which immediately became luminous with phosphorescence, the sea suddenly lit with fairy lights as we splashed each other. Sam and Sarah, doing the crawl, appeared to be escorted by fireflies that danced around them. Lysta gave up cartwheeling along the shore and, with Seth, ran towards us, mesmerised, catching the magical droplets of water that sparkled in their hands.

'Wow, man, have you ever seen anything like it?' said Gregory, scooping up brightly lit handfuls while Ros and Lottie spun around in the waves, creating circles of light. It will stand out in my memory, that night when the Aegean filled us with mystery and wonder.

⛌

The following morning Datsun Jim drove Dinos, Gregory, Lottie and me into Aghios Kirikos.

From the road we could see the ferry steaming towards Ikaria, the sun rising, the shadows shortening. We passed ripening figs ready to be eaten, an abundance of them swaying in the trees. They would be over the top soon if no one picked them. But that's how it was, too much fruit just an arm's length away. They weren't worth trying to sell in the grocers' shops because they were there, in easy reach, for anyone who wanted to stretch out a hand.

Datsun Jim dropped us off and Dinos went in search of

some locals, hoping to persuade them to get off their arses and fight for a good cause. Gregory, Lottie and I sat on the harbour wall watching the ferry dock. I could see a group of nuns on the top deck leaning over the railings. Were they the ones coming to support Sister Ulita? Most of them looked very young, just teenagers, laughing and excited; only three or four appeared to be in their forties. Not really a sight that would instil any fear in Petros.

For many of these girls, it was probably their first trip away from Samos. What followed was something of a calamity, as they walked in single file down the wooden gangway. It couldn't bear the weight of so many people at once and suddenly, with a ghastly cracking sound, it broke in two and three nuns fell into the sea. Others clung to the shattered gangway, one swinging above the water. Members of the crew dived in to carry out a swift rescue as the nuns frantically tried to keep themselves and their suitcases afloat. From where we were sitting, they looked remarkably like a family of seals. One of the cases had burst open and the contents spilt out, various articles of clothing drifting across the harbour waters.

We looked at one another in total disbelief as a controlled pandemonium unfolded around us. The captain of the ferry shouted orders through a megaphone to the crew, who splashed about in the water. While others threw lengths of rope, the sister dangling from the broken structure was heaved to safety.

'If I hadn't packed my camera I'd photograph it,' said Gregory.

'It's hard to be sure this isn't some bizarre comedy routine we're witnessing,' said Lottie.

'Oh, it isn't that,' I said. 'Look at the gangway. The planks are completely rotten.'

All the excitement, if you could call it that, was over in fifteen minutes. Amazingly, nobody appeared to be injured; perhaps the only casualty was the pride of the saturated nuns, who sat on the quayside comforting one another.

Eventually, the outgoing passengers were allowed to board. I asked Gregory what the chances were of receiving a postcard from Egypt. I'd already given him our Poste Restante address.

'Of course, man. A felucca going down the Nile.'

'And you, Lottie, will you send us one from Amsterdam?'

'I will, as soon as I get home.'

I watched them walk gingerly up the new gangway, some quickly erected construction, bits of wood held together with knotted ropes. I left the quayside and walked over to Stelios's mooring. I could see him helping tourists on board, a sign nearby saying *Boat trips 200 drachma*.

'*Kali mera*, Stelios.'

'You see why I am not fishing?' he said. 'It is here before your eyes.'

'I've come to tell you we are leaving the island soon.'

'You are sure? Then before this, we must go fishing, yes, one more time.'

17

Victory

I walked to the monastery wondering what awaited me, how I would be received by an army of nuns. Ros had milked the goats the previous afternoon, and told me all the talk had been about the sisters falling into the sea. Meeting the children distracted them and they were soon playing hide and seek.

I, of course, received a rather different welcome, bashful to say the least. Coy looks greeted me as I walked through the courtyard, where I found Artemis in a tight-fitting dress chasing a rat with a spade.

'The problem is getting worse,' she said, obviously exasperated. 'Not once, but many times a day I see them.'

'You will have to put poison down,' I said.

'And that cat, I keep telling her not to feed it, that it should hunt for its food.'

I remembered we had had the same problem on the farm. Initially I had tried shooting them with an air rifle, but I was a hopeless shot so we put warfarin down. That got rid of them.

'I am going back to Athens. I'm fed up. The place is overrun with rats, and now nuns.'

We heard Sister Ulita approaching, purpose in her step. She took Artemis and me by the hand and led us into the church, closed the door and sat us down. After bowing to the gold cross on the altar, she went straight into a rushed monologue without pausing for breath. Artemis raised her hands. '*Stamatao!*' Stop.

A profound silence fell, no doubt accentuated by our surroundings.

'I suppose I have to translate this madness,' said Artemis, trying to compose herself, her earrings sparkling in the sunlight that poured in through the stained-glass windows. Close by me in a glass case I could see the bones of their revered Saint Adrianos. A single honey bee circled above us. I wanted to open the door and let it out; it had work to do. Artemis spoke slowly and quietly as if the most essential thing was to remain calm in what was proving to be a difficult day for her. It was hard to imagine what her perfect day would be, maybe cigarettes and a book alone on a patio somewhere. In company she was abrupt and had very little patience.

As she gradually told me the plan, I wasn't sure who had devised it, Sister Ulita or the bishop. I knew already that a nun's life was full of self-discipline and self-sacrifice and now realised that, if necessary, the nuns would stand in front of the digger and not move an inch. That was their strategy and would be especially effective if the JCB driver happened to be a God-fearing man. When she'd finished translating, Artemis got up and left the church, probably desperate for a cigarette. I had never seen her so on edge. Her tranquil life at the monastery had certainly been disrupted, but what really agitated her were the rats.

All the nuns and I walked out beyond the monastery walls to where the water flowed, coming from underground as clear as glass. The liquid of life, so vital to everyone on a parched island, and when in short supply, through the dry summer months, so often fought over.

For the rest of the morning we threw stones and pushed boulders into the gully to protect the watercourse. Despite our strenuous efforts, though, our blockade would take a digger two minutes to clear away. The nuns all worked together, their pace never easing, apart from short breaks to drink water from a goat skin.

Sister Ulita sat away from us, a lonely figure on a rock, her arthritic hands clasping a silver cross to her chest. She was lost in spiritual contemplation, or baffled by the great conundrums of life, and the flawed souls who had broken into her divine world. If she ever needed a saviour to turn up, it was now. Again I was struck by my complicated position in the whole drama. Why was I helping to build what was going to be an ugly blot on the landscape? Of course, like the other workers, I needed the job. But I thought of the extra cars it would bring, all the rubbish, the pollution, the sewage and, crucially, the water it was going to require. I felt sure this was the beginning of mass tourism and the end of a way of life. And all the while the monastery's livelihood was under threat. I realised it would be better if the Toula Hotel was never built. All this went through my mind as I watched Sister Ulita concealed behind her sunglasses, hiding those eyes I'd never seen.

🔁

I do not deny that I hoped Artemis would come and find me. For whatever reason, she had not sought me out lately, or had a quiet cigarette watching me milk the goats. Maybe she had withdrawn into herself now that her solitude had been breached and she'd lost the freedom to wander alone in the gardens. And then, as I was picking the first ripe pomegranates in the orchard, I sensed her standing behind me, before she struck a match and exhaled the blue smoke that drifted away through the branches.

It was hard to tell if she rehearsed a single line, but she always began these secluded encounters by saying something that had an undercurrent of tension and intrigue. She said nothing about not seeing me since our lunch together, when she had got drunk on that bottle of wine.

'You know I can read your mind.'

I was certain she couldn't, but I was intrigued by the enticing little journey her words seemed to promise. Could she have come to believe over the summer that I was receptive to her advances, and now be circling before the kill? I didn't want to think I was an open book, prey to this woman who was so clearly experienced in the art of seduction. Rather, I imagined that she was just playing a game, was bored and wanted to amuse herself.

'What am I thinking?' I answered in a tone that implied only mild interest.

'That it is time now for us to swim together.' It came as a complete surprise. I had expected some innuendo and there didn't seem to be any. She just wanted to go swimming.

'I know somewhere that no one knows about,' she continued.

'When?'

'When you have finished your day's work.'

There is an intimacy to swimming with someone on a quiet beach, when there's no one else around, just the two of you, and I admit I wanted to. And yet somehow it seemed deceitful, as if we were secretly stealing away together. But secret from whom? Certainly not Ros; she wouldn't have given my swimming with Artemis a second thought. No, it was as if I was about to be unfaithful to Sister Ulita, and with the temptation came a sense of guilt.

It would have been easier if I could have just slipped away, but Sister Ulita came running towards me, putting a finger to my mouth to indicate I should remain silent while she read from a handwritten piece of paper. 'Good morning . . . and how are you today, sir?'

'Sister, that's marvellous! You have mastered the English language.' And the sheer pleasure this gave her swept across her face, while one of the young nuns came and told me shyly she was teaching Sister Ulita English after evening prayers.

Artemis was waiting for me on the coastal road, carrying a woven bag over her shoulder, wearing sunglasses and a head scarf. She had removed all her make-up; for the first time I could see her natural complexion, her lips thinner, her cheekbones less pronounced.

We passed no one on the five-minute walk and turned down a narrow gap between the great sculptured rocks, just wide enough for one to squeeze through. It was not surprising that this beach was virtually unknown; only the thin would find it, and those who didn't suffer from claustrophobia. We had to step carefully down the sloping, stony track that opened out onto a small stretch of sand where the waves broke gently upon the shore. The hidden cove was no more than fifty yards long, empty and quiet. Only a flock of seabirds scrawled a signature across the sky.

There was a freshness in the air now, warmth no longer carried on the wind, no summer heat burning the skin. Artemis undressed slowly, slipping out of her dress, revealing a black swimming costume. I watched her in the slanting sunlight that gave the shadows a distinct sharpness, her slim figure clearly defined against a deepening sky. She folded her clothes neatly, running her hands over the creases. All I had to do was take off my T-shirt and sandals to swim in my shorts. It seemed as if several minutes had passed before she beckoned me, and together we walked out into the sea up to our waists. Without the slightest splash she glided down into the water, her hair floating over her back, her breaststroke so slow she could turn and say to me, 'Now we are swimming together.'

I knew everything was contrived even before she disappeared below the surface. This stolen swim in the Aegean meant nothing and was going to lead nowhere. She was a solitary, sophisticated woman who I suspected kept her distance from emotional relationships. Maybe this was no more than a distraction from the long summer hours spent embroidering an altar cloth. I had seen the slow progress of the undertaking for myself, the precision of each stitch, the rise and fall of the needle as the two women sat at the table in the courtyard. I'd seen the altar cloth occasionally when they unfolded it, and it looked hardly changed.

After we had swum for no more than ten minutes she walked back up the beach and began drying herself. I didn't have a towel and shivered, pulling my T-shirt over my wet body. She gave me no warning that she would remove her swimming costume, and revealed her nakedness without inhibition. I turned my back; it was I who was embarrassed. When she had finished dressing she said, 'Why can you not look at a naked woman?'

I didn't reply, saying only that it was time for me to go.

As we parted she said, 'I hope you are happy now we have swum together.' As if we had made love, and I should be satisfied.

The taverna was packed; I could hear the noise at least two hundred yards before I got there. I thought it was a wedding party even though it was six o'clock on a Tuesday evening. But nothing surprised me on Ikaria. It was in the islanders' blood to find a reason to celebrate, whether it was a saint's day or someone's birthday. As long as it went on late into the night, wine and music flowing, and everyone, young and old, dancing the Ikariotikos in a large circle beneath the eucalyptus trees, until dawn swept away the last stray stars.

But this was something quite different. Dinos was being carried shoulder high around the taverna and everyone was singing at the tops of their voices, without accompaniment. It sounded like something you'd hear at a sporting event, rousing stuff after a great victory. And it was.

'Petros has conceded,' Angelos shouted into my ear, giving me a hug robust enough to break a couple of ribs. So it had all been worth it. 'He's agreed to everything, including the extra thirty drachma an hour.' They were the words I wanted to hear.

Maria was living every moment of this success, dancing with the others. In amongst them I could see Ros and the children, carried along in the euphoria. The one person I could not see was Datsun Jim, and I was sorry he wasn't there to share the excitement.

When I sat down with Angelos and Dinos and we opened a bottle of retsina they told me that it had been made clear to Petros that the agreement would only last if Zenas stopped his bullying and treated everyone with respect.

'So you've done it. Now we can celebrate long into the night and work with a hangover tomorrow,' I said.

'There was just one condition,' said Angelos, looking away, which usually meant something of a sensitive nature was coming. 'You must understand that we had to agree for everyone's sake.'

'Of course,' I said. 'But what?'

They both looked embarrassed, hesitating, each waiting to see if the other was going to tell me.

'Say it, will you,' I said impatiently.

'You have been sacked,' Dinos told me at last.

'Is that all? Was I the only one?'

'Petros said the Englishman was a troublemaker,' continued Angelos, as if I would take the news badly, which I didn't. 'And your friend Datsun Jim, he also must go, because he is so often late. And the two of you must not set foot on the site again.'

Angelos handed me an envelope that contained three hundred and forty drachma. At least Petros had paid what he owed me. Angelos got up and put an arm round my shoulder, but I didn't need comforting. I was glad for them, and it closed an episode. Once again, I knew it was time to move on.

I'd given up expecting a call from Stelios, so it was a surprise when Maria came over and said he was on the phone.

'We go fishing tomorrow morning, my friend? Yes?' It restored my faith in him.

I left them then to go on celebrating into the night. Ros and the children had already gone home, and I was feeling a bit queasy after a few glasses of retsina on an empty stomach. I sat on the patio watching the trees sway when there was not a breath of wind. Ros came out to sit with me.

'You must feel you've achieved something,' she said. 'I never thought you'd get the better of Petros.'

'Well, I don't know if I did. I've been sacked.'

Ros gave me a resigned look. 'I take it you are the only casualty?'

'No, Datsun Jim as well.'

'Well, that's not surprising, is it?'

'Ros, we must talk about what we're going to do. I think I've made up my mind.'

'Yes, I know, but let me just have one more conversation with Agathi.'

Seth appeared from his bedroom carrying a shoe box, with what looked like air holes punched into the top of it.

'Dad, I have a surprise for you.'

'A dead one, no doubt.'

'No, a live one. It's a lizard. I caught it in my butterfly net. I don't like dead insects any more.'

I was pleased to hear it.

'Can I keep it as a pet?'

'It's not really the sort of creature you can keep as a pet. You'll have to feed it flies all day.'

'Oh, let him keep it,' said Ros. 'He'll look after it, you know he will.'

'I'm going to call it Liz.'

'That's a very good name for a lizard.'

Then he opened the box and held the lizard in his hand. 'Do you want to stroke it, Dad?'

I did, very gently, and then I said, 'I'm going to bed.'

On the way through the kitchen I saw the tape Paulo had given me lying on the table. I slipped it into the cassette player and fell asleep listening to Eric Clapton's beautiful 'Peaches and Diesel'.

⑤

Three days had passed and there was still no sign of Datsun Jim. Maria said I worried too much about the man, when I'd asked her again if she had seen him.

'I've known him since he was a boy. He'll turn up when he needs to eat.'

Maybe he would, but he was back on his own, probably drowning his sorrows in that goat hut.

Agathi had told Ros that there was no money to pay her for teaching English at the primary school in Aghios Kirikos. It was obvious how disappointed she felt. I thought she was clinging to it as a last chance to enable us to stay; for me it reinforced my decision that we should be heading home. I decided to give her the letter from my mother that had been crumpled up in my pocket for over a week.

In it Dinah talked about the new school term that would be starting soon, reminded me we were in fact homeless, and asked where on earth we were planning to live, which I didn't have an answer to. She offered to wire money over to get us back to England. At the end of the letter she wrote in block capitals PLEASE LISTEN TO YOUR MOTHER with a few hurried kisses underneath, and a final sentence: *Jack's going to be a father soon.*

After Ros read it she said nothing about the points my mother had raised and was just annoyed with me for not telling her Jack was going to be a father. But what we had been avoiding was staring us in the face. It was September now and twice in the past week I'd left the taverna to fetch our pullovers; the weather was changing. Most of the tourists had gone; the beaches were thinning out.

'She's right of course,' she said at last. 'Yes, OK, let's go home.'

18

Decisions

The monastery was still full of nuns and despite Sister Ulita's fears no one had come to divert the water, nor had Petros had the audacity to send the JCB to start digging a trench or lay a pipe to the Toula Hotel.

The altar cloth, which was meant to be ready for Saint Adrianos's day, was only half finished. Artemis said it wouldn't be completed for another year.

'That's a lot of *avrio*s,' I said, which she didn't find the slightest bit amusing. All she wanted to tell me was that the rats were taking over and the nuns were going to poison them. She was leaving at the weekend and would not return until the spring. She told me this in a dismissive way, as if I was no longer of any importance to her; maybe the novelty had worn off.

Now summer was coming to an end the sun was losing its intensity, but Sister Ulita still wore her sunglasses, gazing into her shaded world. How can you know someone if you've never seen their eyes? I always felt shut out, even excluded, because of those glasses. We certainly had a friendship and were even fond of each other. I saw it in her attempts to speak English, which had become more frequent since she'd been having lessons from the young sister from Samos. Her confidence had grown; she usually practised when I was leaving at the end of my working day.

'Hello. I think it will rain today,' even though there was no sign of a change in the weather.

To which I replied, 'Yes, I agree, it looks like rain.' I always had to suppress a smile, but these little conversations touched me.

Soon I would have to tell her our plans. That wasn't going to be easy, and it would be a sad day. I felt she had become dependent on me. In all my time working there, no islanders had come to offer help. After I'd gone, who would milk the goats?

That morning Ros was buying the ferry tickets and soon I would know the date of our departure. We really should have been on our way a month earlier, in time for the new school term. It seemed obvious we'd have to stay with my mother, who lived in Westbourne, near Poole, where I had spent my childhood.

I'd booked a call with Jack and hoped the line would be clear enough to be able to talk about other possibilities. As I waited for it to come through, Sarah and I had the taverna to ourselves, sitting over one of Maria's Greek coffees. It was one of the few things I hadn't really taken to, after three sips my lips meeting a dry, gritty sludge. I couldn't understand how the Greeks had allowed it into their culture, these small cups of coffee, served with a glass of water. I would have preferred an instant Nescafe, but they were never that instant, not the way Maria made them, stirring the powder into a paste for many minutes, just as she did the Greek coffee.

Things were much quieter now without the incessant background noise of the cicadas, that great whining tinnitus fizzing in your eardrums.

It was not just Ros and I who were finding it hard to pull ourselves away from the place. I knew Sarah had to return to England to take up her place at Exeter, but no doubt she was wrestling with her heart, not something anyone can help you with. She had never mentioned when she was leaving, and it wasn't a subject I wanted to bring up with her. She and Julia were the only ones left now from the friends we had made during the summer.

How Julia and Stelios had kept seeing each other and sustained a passionate relationship was to be admired, if only for its planning: all their secret rendezvous; Julia's having to swim to shore from the boat.

'What was it you were shouting from the back of the truck when you all came back from the Toula the other day? It sounded something like *korastika*,' said Sarah. 'Is that right? What does it mean?'

'Knackered. I think it first came into my head when I was unloading the potato boat from Samos and now it's just part of my vocabulary. Even Datsun Jim said it the other day.

'You know, I've worked all over the south side of Ikaria and what we had to do at the Toula was hard graft, but there was nothing more exhausting than unloading those sacks of potatoes.'

I heard the phone ring then and Maria called me into her kitchen. For once I could hear Jack loud and clear. My brother had a lot to tell me, not surprisingly as we hadn't spoken for months. He was still working as a shepherd in North Cerney.

'Congratulations. I hear you're going to be a father,' I said. 'And from Ros as well, to the both of you.'

I knew Jack wouldn't want to talk about it, and he didn't, just managing to say, 'Thanks.'

'There are houses to rent here, and Gloucestershire is beautiful. You could get a job on the farm as a stockman.'

'I don't really want to go back to farming.'

'Well, whatever you decide, there's plenty of work, and there's a good primary school in the village.'

'Let me talk to Ros,' I said. 'Any other news?'

'We got married a couple of months ago, in a register office. We didn't invite anyone.'

'And how is Moss?' My border collie, whom Jack had

rescued from a brutal man out in the wilds of Capel Curig.

'She's thriving. She's working every day and sleeping behind the sofa, just like at Dyffryn.'

That was as far as we got, because then the phone went dead as usual, but I'd heard enough to put a plan to Ros: that we should take up Jack's suggestion and join him in Gloucestershire. What was the alternative? Living with my mother? Ros and I had always been close to Jack, and although we didn't really know Corinna, the few times we had met her in Wales we had got on well.

When Ros got back from Aghios, she told me she'd got the tickets and we would be leaving for Piraeus in ten days.

⑤

I was thinking about the plans we'd made when Datsun Jim pulled up outside the taverna. His appearance had changed dramatically again. There he stood in a clean T-shirt, his hair swept back in a new style, his chin shaved, wearing jeans that looked as if they had never been worn before. He undeniably knew how to reinvent himself, I thought, as he embraced me with one of those awful bear hugs. This time I knew what was coming, and managed to breathe in before he clamped me to his chest. Maybe that was another reason Thekla had dumped him, because he squeezed the life out of her. Even Maria was astonished by his appearance and teased him about it, but she was glad to see him. Despite what she'd said, it seemed she too had been worried about him.

'Jim, my friend,' I said, and as soon as the words were out of my mouth I recalled that day of anger when I had shouted at him not to call me his friend. How my feelings about the man had changed. 'What's new in your life? What's happened to you?'

'I am free now of all my troubles,' he said, a gentleness in his voice as if a great burden had been lifted. 'I know the secret of myself.' He leant forward with a sober clarity in his eyes, squeezing my thigh with his bricklayer's hands.

'My friend . . . I can tell you I have found God.' Not a response I was expecting, although I could see Jim was extremely clean, and they say cleanliness is next to godliness.

'Are you certain?' I asked, somewhat flabbergasted. 'How did he come to you? Tell me about it.'

He asked Maria for a Coca-Cola, and after taking a long swig from the can he began the story of the great visitation. My word, not his – he called it a visiting.

He had been in the goat hut one evening as the sky was darkening and the goat had nudged him several times towards the door. It would have been tempting to say 'Maybe the goat was trying to tell you something', but I could see how serious he was. Jim had eventually got to his feet and walked out into the twilight, that special glow just before the night has swallowed up the day.

The actual conversion, from what I could understand, occurred when three shooting stars mysteriously passed overhead within seconds of each other. This cosmic event so overwhelmed him he fell to his knees, and for some reason he read into it an indication that he should follow God. At the same moment, he knew he was over Thekla and no longer needed a woman. He showed all the symptoms of the recently converted, unfortunately including the need to convert everyone around them too. In fact he went on about it for far too long. As he drew breath, I at last managed to get a word in about the victory over Petros and tell him that the two of us had been sacked.

Then I told him that we were leaving Ikaria in ten days. He was so shocked that he fell into a morose silence, eventually saying, 'You cannot leave. This is your home now.'

He launched into a sentimental ramble about the time we had spent together. It was a pity that Ros had little sympathy for him and just thought he had taken advantage of me, which probably he had, but only because of his own incompetence.

'Now I will have to go back and build my brother's house without you to mix the cement.'

'Come on, Jim, you don't need me. You have God now, and that should keep you occupied for a while.'

'Yes, God and a goat. What else does a man need?'

I almost said a woman, but it wouldn't have been appropriate. It was hard to imagine Datsun Jim surviving such a self-inflicted discipline. Maybe Sister Ulita could help him. She didn't yet know she would be needing someone to work at the monastery and milk the goats.

I woke early, before the sun had cleared the haze. The air cooler now, one could walk without a sweated brow. I passed the Toula Hotel; the nearly completed ground floor must have stretched for fifty yards, a long line of bedroom windows without their frames. The arched main entrance was taking shape, the swimming pool now dug out beside the building.

When I got to the boat, Stelios was drinking coffee and smoking a Karelia, his shirt sleeves rolled up.

'Look, for you today,' he said, 'she is a fishing boat again,' pointing to the piles of nets and polystyrene boxes across the deck.

'And you will take her out and be my skipper. Are you happy with this?'

'I am,' I said. 'So, we are going fishing together for the last time.'

'*Ochi.* There is no last time for Ikarians.'

He was in the upswing of a boisterous mood, when life could be laughed at, and whatever confronted him was brushed aside. Throughout the morning his high spirits never waned, and he got more excited as he suggested singing '*Pende pano, pende cato*'. So we did, although I still only knew the chorus. All this exuberance without a drop of alcohol. It was after we had put the nets down and he opened a bottle of retsina that he became contemplative. Lighting yet another cigarette, he finally stopped humming, picked a strand of tobacco from his teeth and spat into the sea.

'I knew a man once,' he said, but didn't finish the sentence, looking away into the distance.

'You knew a man once?'

'I knew a man once,' he continued, 'who had seven children, and after the last child was born he never slept with his wife again.'

'Why not?' But he didn't answer me.

'All of his life he fished the Aegean. They bring up these children, and he looked after his mother and father. This he did for over thirty years.'

'A hard-working man who supported his family,' I said.

'I cannot do it,' he said, pouring himself another retsina.

'This man, he is my father.'

'What are you saying, Stelios?'

'I'm a man who should never have married. I have what you call a weakness for women.'

'Are you telling me your father is an unhappy man?'

He drew in a deep breath, flicking his cigarette butt into the sea.

'*Nem pirasi.*' Never mind. 'Come on,' he said, shaking himself out of his despondency. 'It is the same for all men.' And then he changed the subject.

'You know,' he said, laughing. 'This is me, what you English call "in a nutshell".'

I didn't ask him about Julia, and he didn't mention her once. As we brought in the nets, working together, it all came back to me, the satisfaction of being on a *kayiki*, a small vessel in a vast sea, doing what people have done for thousands of years.

The two of us pulled fish from the nets, throwing the catch into the buckets and polystyrene boxes. This was how I wanted to remember him, out at sea, or when we went night fishing, talking in front of a fire as we cooked barbunia. Or that wild night when I went overboard, and then clung to that engine made in Derby all the way back to Aghios Kirikos.

When we parted, he said, 'My friend, I tell you this. If you want to know someone, go to sea with them.'

🔳

It was Angelos who came and told me that Petros had started to dig a trench leading from the Toula Hotel across the open scrubland. A part of me hoped that we would have left the island by the time he reached the monastery. I could see it all quite clearly, the nuns standing with arms linked in front of the digger.

In three days Artemis was leaving on the Saturday boat to Piraeus; not particularly good timing to be losing our translator. The idea of discussing tactics with Sister Ulita using a phrase book didn't instil me with a lot of confidence.

After an early-morning swim, I returned to the taverna where Dinos was saying goodbye to Maria and Yannis. It certainly was the season of farewells. He had made quite an impression on me that day when we took on Petros, showing fearlessness and strength of character. I wished I had got to know him better.

'I will be back next summer. Maybe then you will taste some more of my Ikarian cooking.'

'Maybe. Let's hope so,' I said, knowing full well we would not meet again.

I could have done with Dinos by my side through what we were going to be facing at the monastery. I watched him walk away, heading for Aghios Kirikos, Maria weeping a mother's tears, Yannis raising an arm above his head, waving a slow goodbye to his son.

I awoke in the middle of the night, filled with anxiety. I didn't want to be going home not knowing what I was leaving behind. I couldn't just walk away from Sister Ulita, feeling I could have done more. No Ikarians would come to her aid, because of all the trouble over the water in the past. She would get no sympathy there, and I dreaded having to tell her we were going home. I looked at Ros sleeping; she didn't know to what degree all this was affecting me.

I got dressed and went and sat in the taverna, remembering all those who had been there through the summer. The eucalyptus trees swayed above me, their branches bending in the Aegean wind. I thought of Artemis, tomorrow being her last day, and how we would say goodbye to each other. Maybe she would just shake my hand, turn away and be gone. I was surrounded by empty tables, staring out to sea. The Aegean was so familiar to me now, the way it mirrored the night sky and invited you to dream its history. At last I told myself I couldn't wait any longer for something to happen. We needed to seize the initiative. There was no other way. Tomorrow I would tell Sister Ulita we had to march on Petros, me and an army of nuns.

⌐

When I arrived at the monastery, Artemis showed me the bodies of two dead rats on a shovel she was holding. She couldn't look at them, telling me to find a spot to bury them as far away as possible. She was wearing a pair of rubber gloves, quite unlike her usually sophisticated self. She made me follow her, pointing out where she had put down little heaps of poison, and one extra-large pile in the pantry, where Sister Ulita kept her cheeses and pots of yoghurt. If I had not been distracted by other things weighing on my mind, I would have paid greater attention, but I was agitated.

I told her that I needed to discuss Petros with Sister Ulita as soon as possible. To emphasise the urgency, I nearly said we were also leaving Ikaria soon, but stopped myself in time.

When Sister Ulita emerged from her morning prayers I asked her to come and sit at the table in the courtyard, scattering the nuns like a flock of rooks. Apart from praying, how did they occupy themselves all day? I only knew they made jam, sewed garments and washed their clothes, which they hung between the cypress trees. One morning I saw them beating carpets with wooden poles, the most strenuous exercise I had seen them take. The rest of the time they seemed to spend walking around the monastery gardens reading prayer books, and coyly smiling at each other.

When Artemis joined us, I told them both that we had to go and confront Petros that day.

'All of us must walk to the Toula building site. And you must tell him he cannot take a drop of the monastery's water. You must show him you will stand up to him.'

I hit the table with the flat of my palm for emphasis and then waited for Artemis to finish translating. Her words were met with no enthusiasm whatsoever, just complete silence. I decided to give the nun a minute and if she didn't agree I would walk away from the island with a clear conscience.

But she didn't need a minute, for a stream of words suddenly poured from her. I had noticed it before, this combustible side to Sister Ulita's nature. Artemis translated for me, deliberately dropping her voice to not much more than a whisper. She said that the sister agreed we should march on Petros, all of us, and that if necessary fifteen nuns would lie in front of his digger.

I also told the sister that I should say nothing, because it was not my argument. Having an irate nun raising her fists would be far more effective than a troublesome Englishman, who was already a thorn in Petros's side. Then Artemis let out a horrified scream as a rat ran over her foot and scurried into a hole in the kitchen wall.

19

The End of Nearly Everything

We could have done with a brass band marching ahead of us. We needed something rousing, not only to help concentrate the mind, but to put a livelier step in what seemed like a leisurely afternoon stroll. Although I suppose in loose-fitting sandals that would have been impossible.

Sister Ulita had insisted we bring the goats, as far as I could gather because she thought they would enjoy a change of scenery. I didn't argue the point. They were held on long lengths of rope that allowed them to graze the verges, or leave the road and eat whatever they fancied, stripping every bush they came upon. One thought she could climb a fig tree and got her rope tangled in the branches, holding us up for at least five minutes.

Ambling along the coast road, we passed the taverna, where Maria and Yannis looked at us in astonishment. I had no idea whether Sister Ulita knew them. I'd never seen them together, but I hadn't forgotten the time when Maria shouted at her as she sped past the taverna on her moped, covering the diners in a cloud of dust.

After twenty minutes we should have been at the Toula building site, but were not even halfway. The sisters seemed more interested in having fun and gathering herbs and figs. No one was the slightest bit concerned about what lay ahead; perhaps they hadn't been told what awaited them.

Then Datsun Jim pulled up and in his typically exaggerated fashion knelt in front of Sister Ulita, kissing her hand as if she were the Mother Superior herself. I was beginning to give up on the day, which was making a mockery of the sleepless night I had gone through. They talked for a few minutes, and then Datsun Jim put the two goats in the back of the pick-up and, with Sister Ulita in the front, drove on slowly ahead of us.

Finally, we arrived at the site gates, where Zenas came to meet us, obviously intrigued by the sight of so many nuns. He even smiled, something I'd never seen in all the time I'd worked on the Toula site. He tried to amuse them with some flirtatious behaviour, bowing and removing his cap, and then with a sweeping gesture of his arm inviting them in. But his mood changed in an instant when he saw Jim and me, and he warned us not to take another step.

'Jim, stay where you are . . . let Sister Ulita do the talking,' I said, reminding him that we had agreed not to set foot on the site again. The difficulty with Jim in these tense situations was that he lacked self-restraint. He threw himself into everything, whether it was God, a woman or a good brawl. He was not Hercules unchained exactly, but certainly unhinged. So I grabbed his wrist and said, 'Jim, don't move.'

But now Sister Ulita, with palms pressed together, came quietly to Zenas in a way only a nun can, with a spiritual calmness. It created a passive setting for an aggressive man to listen with a receptive ear, while around us the building work continued, and all the men we had laboured with waved discreetly behind Zenas's back. He seemed to be listening intently and only occasionally shook his head from side to side. Neither of them raised their voice, and their demeanour was certainly not that of two people discussing something so volatile.

Only after Zenas shook Sister Ulita's hand and escorted her back to the pick-up did I see her tears. As I helped her into the front seat I said, 'Sister, are you all right? What has happened? What did Zenas say?'

But of course she didn't understand. She looked towards the skies, her hands together, holding her silver crucifix to her lips. It was strange seeing her in such an emotional state when there had been no drama, no raised voices, no extreme gestures.

Half an hour later, back at the monastery, it became apparent that the God Datsun Jim had found was of the lenient variety. He started showing off to the nuns, moving the cross that hung around his neck to the front of his T-shirt. Jim wasn't big on subtlety, and he thought this would convince them he was a likeable, pious man whom they'd find interesting. He hadn't grasped the commitment that nuns give to their God. I suspected that for him this religious awakening would be no more than a dalliance until something else distracted him.

'You have done enough for today, Jim . . . I'll see you in the taverna tonight.'

At last I could sit down with Sister Ulita and hear, through Artemis, everything that Zenas had said. He'd told her that Petros had nearly completed the purchase of the scrubland between the hotel and the monastery, and that soon they would begin drilling for water. Apparently, a water diviner had found an underground spring and shown them the exact spot. In a few days, they would bore some fifty metres down and pump the water to the surface. They had already carried out tests and there was more than enough to supply the Toula. Sister Ulita was to have no fears. He had given his word that not a drop would be taken from the monastery.

So had those been tears of joy I had seen, or perhaps extreme relief? Did I believe it? I had to; we were leaving the island in a few days. Clearly Sister Ulita believed it; now in exceedingly good spirits, she continually patted my knee as Artemis translated the story.

She beckoned me to follow her into the church and there she knelt, wanting me to kneel beside her and give thanks. No doubt she saw the resolution of the matter as an act of divine intervention, and nothing to do with the fact that Petros had found another source of water which for him was economically a much better alternative. God had been on her side and had looked after those who were his servants. So I knelt, because I wanted to share the moment with her; after all, it was something we had been through together. As she prayed, with her head tucked into her chest, she spoke only in a whisper, while I was watching particles of dust floating in a beam of light, thinking about when would be the right moment to tell her we were leaving. Her sunglasses had slipped down her nose, but I still couldn't see her eyes, for they were tightly closed.

As I was leaving the monastery, she came to me in her girlish way, pulling once again a piece of handwritten paper from her pocket, reading to me in English, 'Ros and the children, yes will come for lunch tomorrow?'

'Thank you, sister. Yes, they will come for lunch tomorrow.'

Artemis was leaving in the morning. I wanted to be alone with her, if only for a few minutes to say an unhurried goodbye, and try to make some sense out of what had so attracted me to her.

᠁

We had supper that night in the taverna with Sarah and Julia. Ros had already told them we were leaving in a week. They too had decided it was time to go and would be coming on the ferry with us back to Piraeus. Their Greek odyssey and passionate love affairs were coming to an end. Julia had decided to stay with friends in Athens and find work. She wanted to learn Greek and wasn't ready to make her way back to New Zealand. Sarah said Ilias was going to visit her in England and she'd be coming back to Ikaria next year.

Sam and Lysta had been helping Maria by serving on the tables to the handful of diners. A group of German hill-walkers demanded their attention, keeping them busy as the night clouded over. I missed the cicadas, the sounds of summer. It was much calmer now without all the usual noise of the taverna, people singing and dancing, shouting to Maria, wanting to know when their meal would arrive.

Then, almost without warning, a thunderstorm erupted, a vast spectacular display of light over the Aegean, splintering the night, cracking open the darkness. It rained so fiercely that the drops bounced on the tables, while the branches of the eucalyptus trees swayed like the manes of wild horses. The downpour had us running for cover.

In the morning I walked through a ghostly mist to the monastery. I had left earlier than usual, the air damp from all the rain that had fallen. Not just Artemis but the sisters too were leaving today. When I arrived they were already gathered by the gates with suitcases in their hands, milling around like excited schoolgirls going home at the end of term.

I didn't know how to say goodbye to a nun. Did I kiss her on both cheeks? That would be a lot of kisses, and besides, apart from exchanging polite smiles every day, I hardly knew them.

So we shook hands, all of them giving me bashful looks. Had it been like a holiday for them? I'm sure they never knew what had really been going on, the unfolding drama. When Sister Ulita came to say goodbye to them, I slipped away to look for Artemis and found her smoking, sitting on the bench under the pear tree. This was how I would remember her, a woman who always seemed preoccupied, whom no one could get close to. She was wearing a raincoat, the collar turned up, her legs crossed as if she was waiting patiently for a train. The blue smoke from her cigarette floated in the still air, creating an aura against the greyness of the day.

'I have come to say goodbye,' I said. I didn't know what to expect, though I thought it quite likely she would just get up and walk away, as she'd always done when it suited her to end a conversation.

'So you are leaving too. I doubt it's for ever . . . just a parting.'

'No, it's goodbye. I will not be back. I don't think we will meet again.'

'You will not be coming next year?'

'No, we will not be returning to Ikaria.'

She stubbed out her cigarette and turned down her collar. For a few moments we looked at each other, but I could read nothing in that impassive expression, not a sign, not a clue to what she was feeling.

'Well, you can kiss me if you want,' she said, standing up and coming towards me, offering her cheek.

'I have a question,' I said. Not that I expected an answer, but I asked it anyway, because I would have regretted it if I hadn't. I wouldn't have asked anybody else, but there was nobody like Artemis.

'Has anything really been going on between us?'

As soon as the words were out she laughed, and I wondered if it was to hide her embarrassment.

'You are still a boy . . . you do not understand an older woman.' And she touched my cheek with her fingers and gave me one delicate kiss on my lips. Then she walked away into the vaporising morning, as blurred rays of sun filtered through the lifting mist.

Just before she disappeared, she turned back and I heard her last words. 'I let you enjoy me only in your imagination.'

For a few seconds I could hear her footsteps fading away, and then she was gone.

🔄

I didn't join Ros and the children for lunch. I had found a section of boundary wall in the vegetable garden that had collapsed in the torrential rain. I needed to rebuild it, and quickly, otherwise the wild goats that roamed the area would be through it and strip everything in sight. I had repaired countless stone walls in North Wales and it was always back-breaking work, every stone needing to fit precisely. It would take hours and I needed to have it finished before nightfall.

There was a cool breeze coming in from the Aegean. Above me in the distance huge white clouds were swirling up over the ridgeline of the mountains, billowing downwards like an avalanche over the limestone cliffs. For a while I felt as if I was back at Dyffryn, remembering when Jack and I spent days bent double, our backs exposed to the biting winds, Ros rubbing Deep Heat into us later. My thoughts turned to the future, and the direction we'd be taking. We would just have to see when we got to Gloucestershire.

I had been working for a few hours when I heard Sister Ulita's hysterical voice shouting for me. She was out of breath by the time she reached me.

'*Grigora, grigora!*' Quickly, quickly.

Whatever could she want that was so urgent? She was frantic, pushing me forcefully in the back to make me run on ahead.

When I reached the courtyard only Sam was on his feet, crying over Ros who lay unconscious on the flagstones. Lysta and Seth were sprawled nearby, their bodies outstretched as if they had been shot.

'Sam, what's happened?' I said wildly, looking into Ros's half-open eyes. They seemed glazed and lifeless.

'They were eating the cheese that the sister always gives us. I didn't want any.'

'It's the rat poison . . . they've been bloody poisoned!' I shouted into the air. I told Sam to stay with them and ran from the monastery, down onto the coast road, heading in the direction of Xylosirtis, praying I would meet a car that could take us to Aghios Kirikos. I told myself to keep calm, but all I felt was a terrible panic, and then I saw the black BMW coming towards me. Of all the people it could have been, it was the one enemy I had made on the island. I stood in the middle of the road waving my arms. It was impossible for Petros to drive round me, so he had to stop. He wound down his window, aggressively gesturing, as if to slap me away with the back of his hand.

'You fool, you want me to kill you?'

'Petros! Please, I need your help! We must go now quickly to the monastery,' I yelled, jumping in beside him. Seeing the state I was in he obeyed without saying a word, and when we rushed into the courtyard Sister Ulita was wiping Seth's face with a wet cloth, tears streaming down her cheeks, begging my forgiveness.

There was a Red Cross medical centre in Aghios Kirikos, but what facilities it had I didn't know. Petros and I managed to get Ros and Lysta onto the back seat, and Sam sat with them.

'Will they be all right, Dad? They're not going to die, are they?'

I held Seth on my lap and Petros drove like a maniac along the coast road, taking us to the very edge as we rounded each bend. We were only inches away from crashing onto the rocks below, and in those dark moments I handed over our lives to whoever looks after our destinies.

Suddenly, ahead of us, I saw Julia thumbing a lift. I yelled at Petros to stop and pick her up. I needed someone to help me think straight. She squeezed in the back, telling me Ros was foaming at the mouth and felt cold. She held Lysta in her arms until at last we arrived at the little Red Cross medical centre.

I rushed in and found a young nurse who was taking a splinter from an elderly woman's finger. She immediately rang for a doctor and while we waited it felt as though the whole world had stopped. Nothing was happening quickly enough. Petros came to me and, despite all our differences, spoke sympathetically.

'You do not need me now. I hope your family is well soon.'

I thanked him as we shook hands, and I warmed to him. He had shown another side of himself and where would we have been without his help.

In ten minutes a doctor arrived. He examined Ros, Seth and Lysta, made three phone calls and then gave them each an injection.

My name is Dr Papadopoulos,' he said. 'I'll do all I can to help your family.'

Lysta was sick first, soon followed by Ros and Seth. I felt their foreheads, hot and sweaty, while their bodies shivered as if they were freezing. I asked him how they were, what he was thinking. He seemed to have no sense of urgency, just checking their pulses.

'Give it some time for the injection, yes, then we will see.'

Julia wet some flannels and the two of us held them against their faces. Seth was delirious and calling for his mother. Again I confronted Dr Papadopoulos. 'Is there no more you can do?'

'We have to wait, you understand.'

'For how bloody long?'

'I don't know, perhaps an hour.'

'And then what?'

'Maybe we will have to fly them to Athens by helicopter.'

'Let's do it now!' I said. 'An hour might be too late.'

'No, it is too soon. It is difficult, I know, but you must wait. Go and sit down.'

There was nothing I could do, no one I could telephone, no one to turn to, and I raged against our helpless situation in that little Red Cross medical centre. Julia could see the state I was in and put consoling arms around me.

'The doctor is right, we just have to wait. What else can we do?'

Half an hour later Ros started to stir, and the nurse, who had done nothing to this point, got her to take a sip of water. She opened her eyes.

'Ros, talk to me. How are you feeling?'

'Give me some more water.'

Dr Papadopoulos put his hand on my shoulder. 'This is good.'

Lysta too showed signs of coming back to consciousness, muttering, 'Mum, where are you?' She was feeling cooler now and managed to swallow a few drops of water.

As for Seth, from being a dormant heap lying lifeless on the bed, he sat almost bolt upright and stared in silence before he burst into floods of tears. He'd never cried very much as a baby; even when he fell over he would just pick himself up. He was inconsolable for a few minutes, until he saw Ros trying to wave to him from the next bed.

Then Sarah rushed in, out of breath, saying she had passed Petros on the road and he had told her what had happened.

'It's terrible! Is there anything I can do?'

'It's all right. Well, I think it is,' I said.

'I'm not ill,' said Sam. 'I didn't eat any of the cheese.'

'Cheese?' said Sarah.

'Cheese and rat poison,' I said.

After two hours they were on their feet, feeling groggy and weak, but recovering. Julia and Sarah stayed with us all the time, getting them to drink as much water as they could and comforting the children.

Dr Papadopoulos, a man in his late forties whose furrowed brow prevented little beads of sweat from rolling down his face, explained to me what he thought had happened. All the symptoms he had treated were consistent with having eaten rat poison, but only small amounts had been digested. The body's initial reaction is to go into shock, but he was sure this stage had now passed and in the morning the horrible experience would be behind them.

'When can they eat again?' I asked him.

'When they are hungry.'

We all got a taxi back to Lefkada, Julia and Sarah insisting they wanted to stay with us for the evening. Maria and Yannis met us, their deep concern showing on their faces.

'What has happened?' Maria cried, holding Ros's face in her hands.

Ros did her best to explain the whole story to them, while my thoughts were with Sister Ulita. It was too late to go and see her now. I tried to work out what had occurred, how poison had got on to the cheeses. The rats must have picked it up on their feet as they scurried around and then run over the food in the larder. I couldn't think of any other answer.

In the morning, you would never have known what Ros and the children had been through. They'd all slept well and were hungry for breakfast.

When I got to the monastery Sister Ulita came towards me, more like a shadow than a physical being. A lonely figure, her mouth tight and tense, her head bowed, subdued as if defeated by the whole drama of yesterday. With Artemis gone and the sisters all back in Samos, she was alone again. And now I'd come to tell her that Ros and the children were all right but that we were leaving Ikaria in two days. Everyone was deserting her. And I would only be able to do it by stumbling through a basic phrase book, unable to inject any kind of sentiment and with no words of comfort.

We sat at the table in the courtyard, and she handed me an envelope. Inside was a piece of paper, on it a single sentence. *I have told Sister Ulita you are leaving*. It had been written by Artemis. I was pleased that she knew. But now she wanted to say something to me and, following her finger below a few scribbled words, began to read to me slowly.

'I know you are leaving . . . and I am sorry for this to be ending . . . I cry for your family all night.'

That was all, and I knew she couldn't find the words to express what she was going through. I think we both felt the utter frustration of not being able to speak one another's language.

She showed me the larder which was completely empty, scrubbed clean, smelling of disinfectant, no longer stacked with cheeses or jars of yoghurt.

She looked such a solitary figure, standing alone in her Garden of Eden, isolated within her sacred world.

Just as I was about to leave the sun broke through the clouds and I said to her, 'Sister, ever since I have been here, no matter what the weather, you have never taken off your sunglasses.'

She, of course, couldn't understand what I was saying, and just stood there as I carefully lifted them away. And for the first time I saw her hazel eyes, watery from the tears she had shed. It was as if she had suddenly come into being and stepped out from herself and at last I could see what had been hidden for so long. A compassionate heart revealed itself in her kind eyes, a girlish embarrassment in her smile. Her smooth skin showed no line or wrinkle. The shock of the sunlight made her blink and she took the glasses back from me between her arthritic fingers, saying, '*Ochi! Ochi!*'

That was the only time I saw her completely, just for those few seconds, but it was long enough to capture an image of her, and who she was. What had kept her behind those sunglasses, whether she had decided at some precise moment never to show herself to the world, I would never know. The intense emotions of that last morning when I sat with her at the courtyard table made me feel as if I was in some kind of waking trance. Only a half-open window suddenly blowing shut jerked me back to reality.

In the minutes of silence that followed, I don't think I had ever searched so hard for words to try to ease the pain we were both feeling. Surely it would not be possible in any language to tell someone how much you had gained from knowing them and in the very next breath say goodbye.

But that was how it felt, and when she found a crumpled piece of paper and flattened it out on the table top and looked at me and said 'How are you enjoying your watermelon?' I said 'Bravo, Sister!' just as I had before. 'I like the watermelon very much.'

I never saw her again, although I drove to the monastery gates with Datsun Jim on the morning of our last day on Ikaria. I had told him everything about Sister Ulita and the daily routine that was followed in the monastery. That he had his chance now to serve his new-found God, when all I really wanted him to do was look after her and make sure the goats were milked every day. He still didn't believe we were leaving, even though I had told him at least six times, so I said it once more.

'It is not good to go on saying this joke. I will see you later, my friend.'

And now I felt we were friends, and as I watched him push open the monastery gates it struck me that he would not survive anywhere else but Ikaria. The world wouldn't make allowances for such a wayward character, who would always need someone to look after him.

🝰

It was the first time we had ordered a taxi, only because we had more luggage than we'd arrived with; all the stuff we'd accumulated, the children's school notebooks, an Ikarian vase, bits of pottery Ros was taking home as mementos, and of course *Wolf Solent* that Sarah had given me.

On that last day, Seth buried the skeletal remains of his collection of dead insects in the garden. Sam and Lysta carved their initials into the trunk of one of the eucalyptus trees, so small you would have needed a magnifying glass to see them. I wanted to know what the children would remember most from our time here. Sam said, straight away, the day the Ikarian army invaded Lefkada. For Lysta it was her friendship with Xenia. Already they had promised to write to one another every week. For Seth, it was chasing lizards with his butterfly net. Liz had survived in his (her?) box for two days before Seth had been persuaded to release him, but it was clear that a life without pets was not going to be on the cards when we got back to England.

In the taverna for the last time, empty now, we said goodbye to Maria and Yannis. No one had given us more. It was hard to pull the children away from Maria, who didn't want to let them go. She had been like a grandmother, spoiling us all with her treats.

'I will keep on living so I can see you all next year,' were her last words to us.

As for Yannis, probably the most reserved man on the island, he hugged us all, even me.

The taxi was nearly half an hour late – what else should we have expected – but I had allowed for it. We drove with the windows open, breathing in the sea air, staring across the Aegean to the island of Fourni in the distance. Every now and then we caught a whiff of thyme and the distinctive scent of fig trees. The day was pearlescent under nimbus clouds.

How many times had I walked this road to Aghios, whether to go fishing with Stelios, or unload the potato boat, or go in search of Sam? All of us were unusually quiet, caught up in our memories.

Ros had arranged with Agathi to meet at the Casino café, overlooking the harbour. They were the family we had grown closest to. Many friendships had been formed between us, apart from Seth and Leftari, who seemed wrapped up in their own worlds. They knew more about the situation we were facing when we returned home than anyone else, but it didn't stop us from inviting them to visit us in England. Lysta was in the same state as when she said goodbye to Eleri and was now demanding that we stay in Ikaria. No matter what, we all agreed we'd keep in touch. Vassili even said I could take him to a cricket match.

As we boarded the ferry I could see Stamati sitting at one of the café tables. Did he know we were leaving? I was sure Stelios must have told him. He was the first Ikarian we had met. It seemed a long time ago.

We found Julia and Sarah on the upper deck, together with Ilias who had somehow climbed aboard. He'd have to dive into the Aegean, for the ferry had already left the quayside, and he did, in spectacular fashion, before we were out beyond the harbour walls.

Through a choppy sea of white waves we watched the island of Ikaria gradually disappear from view. Was that Stelios's boat I could see? Maybe not. I thought about Sister Ulita and what she might be doing. Did Jim milk the goats this morning? I put my arms round Ros, and said, 'Another episode of our lives behind us, another one about to begin.'

We were going home. Going home to what, I thought, and where is home exactly? We didn't have one. Already I was beginning to look forward to a new beginning.

'Nick, I think I'm pregnant.'

I didn't know what to say, so made light of it. 'Jim's grandmother's bed has a lot to answer for.'

'Dad,' said Sam, with that expression that told me something deep was coming. 'I don't know why I want to do it, but I have to.'

'What are you trying to tell me?'

He opened his hand and showed me one of the empty cartridge cases he had found left behind by the Ikarian army at Lefkada.

'Why are you showing it to me?' I asked.

'I want to throw it into the Aegean.'

'Go on then, throw it overboard.'

He did, and we barely saw a splash, but for Sam it was as if this act carried some magical significance. Maybe he thought he was leaving something behind that would remain for ever.

'Don't tell anyone, Dad. It's our secret.'

Epilogue

In 2016, Arabella (Sarah) and I returned to Ikaria, thirty-nine years after we had lived on the island. Many twists and turns later, and twenty-five years after we'd met, Arabella and I had married. We'd often thought about going back, knowing it couldn't possibly be the same. How the inevitable changes might well be terribly disappointing and we would wish we'd never gone. You can't return to your past, capture again what a place meant to you, how you were feeling then. Everything moves on, even Ikaria.

It now has an airport, a modest set-up, carved between two hills on the northern point of the island. We flew in on an Olympic Airways flight from Athens that took under an hour, not the eight it takes from Piraeus on the ferry. On the plane, two Ikarian women beside us were nervous. When I asked why, they said it was the wind. Sometimes it isn't safe for the planes to land. 'They shouldn't have built it here, at the end of a natural wind tunnel between the hills.'

Our hire car, a little red Peugeot 305, was covered in small dents and scratches, and when I pointed them out to the girl she said '*Nem pirasi*' and told us the engine was good. The clock showed 120,000 kilometres.

We had decided to stay in Armenistis, on the north side of the island, partly because in 1977 we had lived on the south. We thought that if it had changed dramatically we could retreat north and not go back. The best beaches are here and so is most of the development for tourism, but thankfully there are no high-rise buildings and the landscape is as we remembered it.

After a few days, we headed south to find the past.

It was an hour and a half's drive to Aghios Kirikos and we had to cross the backbone of the island. Out there in the wild hardly anything had changed. There were very few new houses, and it had the look of Ikaria as it was in the 1970s. One thing was noticeable: the increase in the number of cars, which the Ikarians drove into the ground and left to rust on the roadside, along with fire engines and trucks. There is no facility on the island to dispose of old cars, though apparently every few years they are collected and taken by boat to Piraeus to be crushed; but this costs money that Greece certainly doesn't have.

Aghios Kirikos didn't seem to have grown dramatically. All the sycamore trees in front of the tavernas and cafés around the harbour had gone, replaced by masses of tables under pergolas. Although the protected harbour was bigger, there were fewer fishing boats now, maybe half a dozen. I couldn't pick out Stelios's boat, but after all these years he would probably have replaced it, if he was still fishing.

We weren't able to track down Datsun Jim, finding out eventually that he had gone to live with his brother in America. That would have been something, to have met him again. As for Stamati, he no longer ran his restaurant, but still lived in Aghios Kirikos.

Stelios is a big personality and the owner of the first café we went to knew him well and phoned him. Twenty minutes later he appeared, in jeans and a T-shirt. The walk had changed, the thick hair was greying, with each step he swayed, but it was Stelios all right, lighting a cigarette, still smoking Karelias.

We didn't know how to greet each other. I just smiled, and he circled round me, said, 'Yes, it is you,' and finally we embraced. Then we sat and talked for two hours. I couldn't believe it when he said he was still living with his wife. 'We have an arrangement.' He told me Theo had just married for the fifth time and made his living as a pig farmer.

He showed me his boat, another one he'd named *Panagia*,

which he'd bought five years ago, and we agreed that before I left we would go fishing again, the two of us out in the Aegean. I sang '*Pende pano, pende cato*' as we walked back along the quayside, both of us laughing.

Stelios rang Ilias and within the space of a couple of hours we had our second reunion. The Pharaoh, now greying and bearded, walked with a stick, still recovering from a motorbike accident in 2013. He told us about the fire of 1993 that had swept through a good part of the island, including Lefkada. Maria and Yannis, of course, had died years ago.

I asked him about the Toula Hotel; it had closed down three years after opening, Petros having left the island heavily in debt. Apparently it was still up for sale if anyone wanted to buy it.

We drove out of Aghios Kirikos, the road tarmacked now, and could see the shell of the building through bolted wire gates.

And then there we were, back at Lefkada. Where all the tables and chairs had been was now overgrown with dry grass. The green door and shutters on the building at the top of the steps were locked, just visible through overgrown bushes. Maria's little kitchen was derelict, full of leaves, the whitewashed walls faded. I stood exactly where the telephone had been, the cable hanging from the wall, its wires exposed. The eucalyptus trees were still there, much bigger, as majestic as ever, and the cicadas too, high-pitched and filling our ears.

The house where I had lived, beside the taverna, was done up and in good condition. We knocked on the door, but nobody answered; they were probably all down on the beach. We stayed for half an hour, Arabella sketching, while I crossed the road to that hidden path down to the hot springs.

Now, half concealed in a bush, there was a wooden plank, and painted on it the words *Hot Springs* with an arrow underneath. It would seem the Ikarians were only a little more interested in advertising what the island had to offer than they had been forty years ago.

What I would find at the monastery filled me with nervous expectation. It looked just the same as we drove up to those large green gates. I rang the bell and heard it ring out behind the walls, its tone just as I remembered. The nun who greeted me with a gentle smile and welcomed me in was Sister Evniki. Time had stood still here, everything just as before. The cypress trees in the courtyard, the old slate table where I used to sit with Sister Ulita, the bougainvillaea by the kitchen window. Sister Evniki spoke good English and was enthralled when I told her about the time I had spent working at the monastery. She asked if I would like to see Sister Ulita. I couldn't believe that she was still here and I would meet her again. So I followed her through the olive trees, out into the orchard where two goats were still tethered, and then up the steps behind the old outhouse. And there we stood, the two of us, before her grave, a white marble headstone with a Greek inscription which read *Now at Peace in the Arms of the Lord*. Sister Ulita had died of cancer in 2012, aged eighty years. Those were sombre moments. I could hear her calling me, not once but twice, as she always did. Neeko, Neeko.

The following morning I met Stelios at six to go fishing. He let me take the tiller as we left the harbour. He told me how much had changed since the 1970s. Fish stocks had plummeted and he caught very few barbunia. Often he would come back with no squid or octopus. The dolphins had become a big problem, stealing fish from the nets.

'Now the dolphins are protected, but no one protects the fishermen,' he said.

But it was wonderful to be back there with him.

Ikaria is still an enigmatic island. It escapes definition, so through metaphor we tried to conjure up who she is. Someone said they thought she is like a badly dressed, beautiful woman, or maybe she just never bothers to put on her make-up. But whoever she is, we lived a life there once and got to know its people.

On our last evening, we stood on the coast road in front of Lefkada and watched the colours of the sunset fading into the Aegean. The island hadn't changed as much as we had feared, and the view from the taverna certainly hadn't changed at all. Staring into the distance, I remembered how Stelios once said to me, 'I see it in you, the dream of Ikaria.'

Acknowledgements

There are many people I would like to thank for helping me complete *Escape to Ikaria*. Judith Mather, Nathaniel Mobbs, Mike and Jo Saffell. My children, Sam, Lysta, Seth and Belah and of course Jan Perry. Jackie Elvery, Lucia Dhillon, Barbara Hennell and Sarah Gooch whose enthusiasm never wavered, despite all the telephone calls. Heartfelt thanks to Paul Sharpe and Ruth Cleaver.

Greg van Reil, who came back into our lives and relived the memories of those days forty years ago and joined us recently from Toronto to film the promotional clips for the book. Penny Barnett, who lives in New Zealand and trawled through those distant memories to give her version of events. Sister Evniki from Samos for her listening ear, who told me what happened at the monastery in the intervening years. And several Ikarians who played a part in the story: Father Leonidis, who now tends the garden where I once worked, Stelios, Nikos Avagiani and of course Ilias Moraitis who also helped us with the history of the island.

Without the creative efforts of editor Nancy Webber and designer Teresa Monachino and, as always, the undying commitment of Neville Moir and Alison Rae at Polygon, the book would never have reached the printed page. And a huge thank you to Arabella, who not only worked tirelessly on the book, but also reminded me of so much about our lives on Ikaria that could easily have been forgotten.

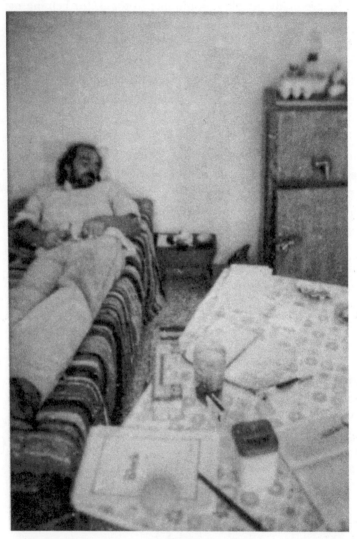

Korastika!